W9-BRY-058

On the
THRESHOLD

On the
THRESHOLD

Home, Hardwood, and Holiness

Elizabeth J. Andrew

A Member of the Perseus Books Group

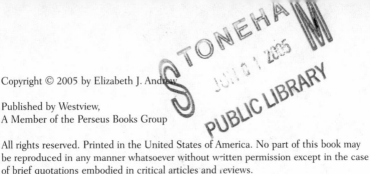

Grateful acknowledgment is made to the following for permission to reprint previously
published material:

"Beggars to God," *Out of Line*, Fall-Winter 2002.

"Praying in Place," *Many Mountains Moving*, Spring 2002.

"On Shining Rails," *Fourth Genre*, Fall 2001.

"Swimming," *Re-Imagining Quarterly*, May 2001.

"Through the Dark Night," *ProCreation*, Spring 2000.

"Room for the Imagination," *Florida Review*, Summer 1999; abbreviated version in
    The Christian Century, August 26-September 2, 1998.

Find us on the world wide web at www.westviewpress.com

Westview Press books are available at special discounts for bulk purchases in the
United States by corporations, institutions, and other organizations. For more information, please contact the Special Markets Department at the Perseus Books Group, 11
Cambridge Center, Cambridge, MA 02142, or call (800) 255-1514 or (617) 252-5298,
or e-mail special.markets@perseusbooks.com.

The paper used in this publication meets the requirements of the American National
Standard for Permanence of Paper for Printed Library Materials Z39.48–1984.

Designed by Jeff Williams

Library of Congress Cataloging-in-Publication Data

Andrew, Elizabeth, 1969-
    On the threshold : home, hardwood, and holiness / Elizabeth J. Andrew.
        p. cm.
    Some material previously published in various publications, 1998-2002.
    ISBN 0-8133-4296-1 (alk. paper)
    1. Home. 2. Homeowners—Biography. 3. Andrew, Elizabeth, 1969- 4. Spiritual
life. I. Title.
    HQ734.A563 2004
    643'.1—dc22

                                                                    2004019328

05 06 07 08 / 10 9 8 7 6 5 4 3 2 1

Contents

᷿

On the
THRESHOLD

Firm Foundation

Inspiration and Vision was then,
and now is, and I hope will always be,
my element, my eternal dwelling place.

William Blake

Entrance

THE BACKDOOR TO THIS HOUSE opens into the pantry. Coming in from the yard, I face shelves overcome with jars: oregano, paprika, and curry roosting in vast extended families; beans, rice, lentils, and bulgur paling in the sunlight; the baking clan (unsweetened chocolate, a jug of honey, coconut, lugubrious molasses, crocks of sugar and flour) awaiting the release of their internal chemistry. Here is the bin for garlic, onions, and potatoes, sprouting their primal appendages. Here are cans of tomatoes and mandarin oranges and coconut milk. Here are the boxes (bright red) of macaroni and cheese. Outside, the garden is wending its weedy way toward zucchini heaven, while inside the ingredients sit, prepared to receive their summons. They will become whatever we make of them.

Crowding the floor is evidence that some already have—the compost bucket, the recycling, the garbage. Behind the open door sits the cat's litter box. Only my closest friends and the neighbor kids come in this way; it's too crammed, too messy.

Rings of olive and vegetable oil stain the shelves. The floorboards are tracked with mud, and usually there's a cast-off pair of sneakers in the doorway. Still, it's my favorite way to enter my little south Minneapolis bungalow, which has been home for four years now. I often ask myself what it means to be *at home*, in the fundamental sense of feeling rooted, of being deeply at ease. The pantry seems as good a way into this question as any. On the west wall hangs a row of pegs, from which dangle a straw gardening hat, a bag of clothespins, and a feather duster. Cobwebs drift along the ceiling. The pantry is a tight space, well trod, packed with potential. As I enter, the screen door slams behind me. No other sound is as welcoming.

Four years ago, when I reached the cusp of age thirty, my need for a house suddenly became biological—a possible exaggeration except I didn't desire a house so much as to settle into myself, and I had no idea how to do that without a foundation, flooring, walls, and a roof. I wanted to be at home in the world and took the obvious route. So I bought this 1930s bungalow from my friend Frank and moved in. Since then my nesting instincts have intensified. I need my window box with its lavish purple-wave petunias and fuzzy silver licorice as urgently as I need morning prayer. Without a dining room table (its extra leaves stacked in the attic), how would I otherwise trust my openness to companionship? A teakettle, with its domestic whistle, pours out a measure of reflection, and the asparagus, which takes five years to establish itself in the garden, helps me set down roots. My mother's quilt flung across the bed returns me to that warm, primary place of comfort, and I can therefore trust enough to release myself into sleep. Surely a sense of spiritual groundedness isn't dependent on lath, plaster, and old, warbled glass. Yet in my material world I crave these assurances.

Just inside the kitchen is what my neighbor Annie calls the "give back" stool. Originally meant for friends to sit on while I cook, it's become the dumping ground for borrowed books, keys, and papers that need to return to their owners. This unruly pile, along with the bags to haul to the alley on trash day, makes the pantry a place of transition—out with the old, over and over.

For years I've floundered as my former understandings of God (parental, omnipotent, theistic, held pedestal high) have gone out with the compost, and I'm left mucking around in the dirt looking for holiness. I no longer know what is sacred, what is not, and how to relate to it all. How does one worship the pervasive pulse of life, the seasons' spinning, the pantry's potential? Prayer has been turned inside out, so the words I used to send toward heaven now might as well be spoken to my own mysterious heartbeat, and the guidance that used to come clearly has receded into an indiscernible but beneficent hum. Perhaps words are best forsaken for silence, which seems to be creation's lingua franca. Where I used to ache to see God's face, I now long to be comfortable in my own—to recognize the sacred mark here, in this city, between walls of stucco and within walls of skin.

So I dig down into the details I *do* know: these jumbled jars, these bags of trash. The Christian mystics say we've already been given everything we need to know God, and I'm testing this idea since the alternative is too daunting. Certainly I've been given everything I need to cook a meal—weeks of meals, in fact; I take comfort in having enough. Although not too much. My stock is not desperately hoarded against disaster, nor is it extravagance. It's just basic plenitude. In an emergency, there's always a can of tuna and some alphabet pasta. My collection of dry goods doesn't evidence any culinary skills so much as a love for translucent grains of rice, brittle strands of spaghetti, and the shriveled red hides of sun-dried tomatoes within glass jars. The hard beans, black and navy and pinto, feed me with their beautiful waiting bodies long before I pour them into the pot. Abundance greets me each time I enter the house, and I respond with reverence.

Anything at all can become the stuff of a spiritual life. This jar of Plondke's sorghum, for instance—where the heck did it come from? And what am I supposed to do with it? The label is stained with age; a tarlike substance coats the glass. Is sorghum some sticky revelation waiting among my more familiar ingredients? Or is it another item I've clung to unnecessarily and ought to ditch? In the corner, Rhia, my longhair calico, props herself on the watering can, dips in a paw, then licks her upturned pad. I worry that the fertilizer I feed the plants will make her sick, but it's what makes watering can water so much more enticing than the fresh water in her bowl. Can I trust Rhia not to drink what's not good for her? Can I trust my own desires? I ought to mop the pantry floor; I ought to give the floorboards a fresh coat of paint. The easy way into the house gets overused and requires more care as a result. The same holds true for well-worn beliefs, the sacred abstractions that I use without thinking. I need to pay closer attention. I need to read what's blatant and patient and already here.

This is my spiritual discipline, this reading of my house for heart and meaning. Of course I plug away at more traditional means, attempting meditation every morning, occasionally struggling with sacred texts, attending my liberal urban church where I fidget through the sermon. When I envision what it might look like to be spiritually *at home*, I see a Sufi master with sturdy, blazing eyes or a Catholic sister who has spent her life in prayer—enlightened beings, recognizable by their calm aura and selfless commitment. I've never actually met individuals that pure, but I hope they exist. It would comfort me to know that devotion to the disciplines of any religion can lead to self-knowledge, faith in one's goodness, and confidence in the universe's inner workings. Unfortunately, devotional holiness isn't practical for me. I don't know how to pray, although I try. I'm too bound to the world, to the delights and foibles of the flesh, to a feminist unraveling of tradition, to my mortgage. I love my cat and my claw-foot tub too fiercely to ever follow an ascetic path.

I wish it were otherwise. I have deep affection for the roots of Christianity, the religion of my upbringing. The model of Jesus' life gives me strong moral guidelines, a passion for social justice, and an example of living by love. I emulate him as best I can through my work as a freelance writing teacher and spiritual director, helping others tend and heal their stories. Liberal Protestantism demands that I bind my life to service. I suspect this is in part because Jesus' story is an outward story, the actions and words of a man as seen by his followers. What's missing from my tradition, however, is insight into his internal life—how he changed his mind about healing the Canaanite woman's daughter after she cried, "Even the dogs eat the crumbs that fall from the master's table!"; how difficult it was to escape the incessant crowds for a quiet place apart; how he made sense of God's seeming abandonment at the cross. When he knelt to pray, what exactly went on inside that man's head? If I had his internal story, I might translate more fully his good model into my complicated life.

But I don't, and instead find myself reading the book of the world for relevant clues. Surprisingly enough, this inclination is also in keeping with Christian tradition. The concept of *liber mundi* arose in medieval monastic communities as a means of recognizing God's handwriting still unraveling in nature. Creation itself is a sacred text, its language resonant with symbol and silence. There's no one-on-one correspondence between the tangible world and any ineffable import residing behind it, and yet I've found that paying attention yields insights. Even my drab Methodist roots teach that human experience is a stage for God's revelation. Were I honest, however, I'd have to admit that these are Christian justifications for what I would do regardless, because it brings me such delight. On the top shelf of the pantry are the mung beans, the alfalfa and broccoli seeds, ready at any moment to sprout white tails and crisply enter my salads. All it takes is a few splashes of water and a week of growth. Is there anything more worthy of meditation?

Long before I thought to live here, Frank, the owner and a friend of mine, described to me what poor condition the house was in when he bought it. "Everything was needy," he said. "The backdoor had never been treated or painted. It soaked up ten coats before it finally was satiated. The past owners had taken and taken and never given back." Dark-haired, stocky, and practical, Frank is an interior designer with a penchant for fixing up old houses. He gave two years to this bungalow, a new roof, new furnace, new appliances, and a new, antique bathroom sink. He painted everything. "You have to put yourself into a good relationship with a building in order to live well there," he told me. I still ponder his words as though they are a formula for finding my place in the universe. The backdoor is holding up, but the pantry floor is not. Rhia's water dipping has, over time, caused the paint to buckle and peel. After four years of riding on Frank's hard work, I'm finally discovering how much effort this relationship demands. There's the basic need for housekeeping (the lids of jars are sticky with dust; kitty litter has been enthusiastically scattered) and, beneath that, upkeep of floors and walls, plumbing and heat. Not to mention any serious improvements I might consider. Putting myself in good relationship with the house and, by extension, with my neighborhood, is an overwhelming, endless task. Unlike the more abstract spiritual disciplines, learning to live well here is a tangible chore, one with both visible and invisible results.

I shake out the mud-caked welcome mat; I sweep up the dirt. Certainly my desire to be grounded in a place and therefore in myself isn't unique. Even the most restless among us (vagrants, suburban executives hiring moving vans every two years, the vast population of twenty-year-olds hitchhiking the globe) yearn to be at ease in the world, to be fully satisfied with ourselves. I understand this as a spiritual longing because I cannot detach the sacred from the self. Home, the tortoise teaches, we carry with us. Surely the ultimate home exists, not in some starry afterlife but here, in how I inhabit the kitchen, with its dust and dry goods and sprouting onions. My poor housekeeping and limited income keep me from the trap of believing that contentment comes with perfection. My ceilings will never be free of cobwebs; I will never own a first-rate shelving system for my canned goods. I cannot make the assumption (which advertising preaches so loudly) that having everything *just so* will satisfy my needs. I'm forced to explore the alternatives. How can I put myself in a healthy relationship with this pantry? What changes can I make to bring more peace into meal making—move the microwave onto a pantry shelf? Learn to not feel shame at my shortcomings? Only a small part of being at home is the home itself. The rest is the being, the creature who dwells, and the very nature of our dwelling.

The dry ingredients are ready. The recipes, handwritten on index cards, are in a box in the kitchen. If I want to make soup, I must go out to the garden or around to the corner store for zucchini or tomatoes or milk. The recipes, many of which are my grandmother's, are trusty guidelines, but to satisfy my taste buds' desire for flair I must improvise with the seasonings. Here is the cast-iron pot; here the wooden spoon, the salt shaker, the gas stove. I turn up the heat. Surely the beans have been eager for just this moment! Or is this a projection of my own eagerness, to soften at the edges, to return to some original, yielding form that dry theology has drained from me? The soup is tumultuous; the vegetables tumble forward, releasing their tender, earthy scent. In the dining room are the table and chairs, the blue bowls, the tapered candles. I strike a match. No home gives as much solace, no meal tastes as savory, partaken in solitude as with company. You, dear reader, are the missing ingredient. I'll leave the back-door open.

Bloodroot

BEFORE I BOUGHT THIS STUCCO BUNGALOW I lived in the north woods of Minnesota and grieved daily what I would soon be leaving—sharp constellations at night, goldfinches at my window, the two-toned arch of freight train whistles, and, first thing in the spring, bloodroot blooming against the forest loam. Surely the wild blossom had been banished from paved Minneapolis. I couldn't imagine home without that delicate, white surprise.

One afternoon, I walked down what would become my front steps and headed east toward the Mississippi, trying on the neighborhood, looking for confirmation that I belonged; I cut down to a paved path skirting the river gorge, with the downtowns of Minneapolis and St. Paul ten miles up- and downriver, and found there, scattered amid rusting cans and last autumn's decay, bloodroot! Each white petal was fleeting and perfect. Their wide green gloves caught the sunlight. The flowers where

I least expected them were a sign from heaven: a trail of white light leading me home.

In the years since then I've come to believe that curling leaves, kicked stones, or drops of river water don't need divine prodding to become messengers. Had the bloodroot not been blooming that day, a flock of raucous crows might have spoken to me instead. My desire for home would have planted its own clues, regardless, between cracks in the sidewalk or among the sprawling roots of oak. White breath scattered in the humus is just one beauty I've sunk my love into; love and this longing for love compose my path. God is diffuse and commensurate, like the black midwestern soil. Desire—our own—seeds the earth, sending down its blood-red roots.

Room for the Imagination

"**Y**OU SHOULD KNOW THERE'S A GHOST in the basement." My friend Frank leveled me with his eyes, checking for my reaction. I gave him my best unsurprised face. "She's a good spirit, but she occasionally scares the dickens out of my cat. You'd have to cater to her whims."

It was April 1998; Frank was preparing to move southwest, fleeing Minnesota's snow, and was ready to put his south Minneapolis bungalow on the market. He had expressed a willingness to negotiate directly with me if I was interested, and I was. The house was trim, a tidy 734 square feet, with a flat yard twice that size and a full-grown spruce angling off the northeast corner. After three years of living in an intentional community in the north woods, I was eager for some solitude in the city. A house of my own, with sturdy, insulated walls, would help me feel settled. The low hum of activity in Minneapolis would keep me connected. Frank had bought the house two years prior with the intention of fixing it up and selling, and the bright walls, spanking white kitchen stove, and new posts boosting the primary cross-beam in the basement were inviting for a first-time homeowner. I imagined myself opening kitchen cupboards and raking leaves; I imagined chatting idly with the neighbors. The possibility of making Frank's house into my own made me eager and restless.

I knew enough not to be impulsive about house buying. Before my stint with communal living, I had considered purchasing a carriage house behind a Victorian in my church's neighborhood. From the outside, the carriage house was hardly notable— a two-story clapboard painted pale yellow. The front porch sloped. The house was perched at the top of a steep hill, so that from the living room you peered through oak treetops out over the silvery Minneapolis skyline. I fantasized about writing on sunny mornings in that urban tree house. The inspector I hired scowled at the odd angle of the second-story floors. He knelt in the center of the bedroom, placing his pencil on the floorboards, and it rolled six feet toward the outside wall, gathering speed until it thwacked against the molding. "Let's go down to the basement," he said gravely. Down in the shadows, he pointed his pencil at the piles of rock without mortar lining the perimeter. "See this?" he said. "No foundation. This isn't a house; it's a garage, and it's sinking." No matter how enchanting it might have been to write among the treetops, I decided, it wouldn't do my soul much good to live in a house without a foundation.

In contrast, Frank's house seemed solid: one story on a straight city street. The floor of the porch was painted in thick red coats. Standing in the living room with all the doors open, I could see into the porch, the front bedroom (nine feet by eight), the back bedroom (nine by ten), the bathroom, up the attic stairs, and into the white kitchen. That was it. Everything appeared to be straightforward. When I hired the inspector again, he pressed his cheek against the basement wall to check for bowing, pointed out a few cracks, and moved on. The basement floor was marked with the broad circumference of the former furnace, a coal-burning monster later converted to gravity gas. Frank had removed it after seventy-three years of service. In its place he put a skinny, forced-air natural gas furnace. The building inspector dismissed the foundation and instead pranced around the furnace, thrilled by the quality of its installation. The wiring was new. The plumbing was copper. It was likely that this foundation was trustworthy.

Except for the spook. Frank became convinced of the ghost's existence when he fixed a lamp over the washer and dryer and the next day found it unplugged, removed from the wall, and set on the floor. "I don't think she likes light," he told me. At first he wasn't sure of her gender, but one day it became clear to him, as though she wanted to be identified. Other than the lamp incident, he felt her to be benign. She lurked, a mild-mannered and comforting presence, in what used to be the coal room. Every morning when he went downstairs to feed his elderly cat, Bailey, he talked to the ghost as though a part of his restoration responsibilities was to make her feel welcome. Perhaps, he reasoned, if he could put her at ease, she might pass on to a more peaceful state.

I supposed it was possible. Back in the coal room it was utterly dark until Frank yanked a string and the corner shocked into view. Cobwebs stretched overhead. The cast-iron trapdoor, which the coal man had swung open to shovel black gold into the house's bowels, had long since been sealed shut. Along the north wall were shelves for pickle jars, or, in more recent years, cans of paint that left their sticky, colored rings. Frank didn't want to sell the house unless he was sure the next owner would treat the ghost with courtesy. "She was here first," he said. I nodded, pretending to follow his logic. The air was damp, the quiet dense. I made a sincere effort to perceive what was not obvious. Was I psychically impaired, my imagination too small to permit a ghost's existence? Or was Frank off his rocker? Bailey, otherwise decrepit, suddenly bolted up the stairs and spent the remainder of the afternoon under Frank's bed. Perhaps Bailey sensed what I, with my thick skull and thicker beliefs, could not.

Now I laugh at Frank's peculiar prerequisite and the way his sweet house soon overshadowed my home-buying ventures. It's interesting to me how seriously I struggled with whether or not to believe in Frank's ghost. Now I'm more intrigued by what difference such a belief might make. The structures we heave up around life's mysteries—religious traditions, for instance, or superstitions, or the towering explanations of science—eventually reveal themselves to be inadequate, and yet without them we have no framework within which to dwell. A house with a ghost in its basement (rather, an owner who believes this is so) makes me ponder how humans build frameworks around the unknown so that we may encounter it safely.

When Carl Jung's patients dreamed of houses, he understood the image to signify the soul, with its many rooms, windows, and shadowed eaves. During the months I spent making my decision, Frank's white molding and snug bedroom appeared in my dreams. I floated from room to room, preoccupied, the house simply a backdrop for vague, slow-motion dramas. During my waking hours, I fretted that buying the first and only house I'd seen was too impulsive for such a huge investment. So I found a realtor and toured little working-class houses throughout south Minneapolis. Their basements were shifty places, prone to flooding, disparaging of light, home to cobwebs and unnatural, mechanical moans. Furnaces, cement floors, insulation, plumbing, electrical wiring, gas hookups, floor drains, support beams, coal chutes, heating ducts, concrete blocks, bare bulbs with pull chains. Uneven staircases. Window wells and unwashed windows. What kind of foundation would it take to support a healthy spiritual life? I considered these many basements as though the standard for home buying lay in the foundation. I wondered whether it was possible be selective about what house appeared in my dreams, or if my psyche had already decided.

My means for choosing a house seemed peculiar until I remembered my childhood home, and how it was a metaphor we moved into—suburban ticky-tacky against the Hudson's broad current, the clear-thinking light of the upstairs supported by a dank basement. Our Tarrytown house was a 1950s split-level with a wide bank of windows embracing oaks and tulip trees, a stretch of wetlands, the commuter line rumbling into New York City, and the wild expanse of the Hudson. The view erased the house. All that water filled our living room with dappled sunlight. My young parents were eager to fit into the moneyed, Westchester neighborhood, and at the same time they revered natural beauty with an unaffected religious passion. In the public places of our house, cleanliness and order were strictly enforced. Creative freedom, inner shadows, and dust were relegated to the basement.

The Tarrytown basement was partially finished, with a perpetual damp smell. The iron railing in the stairwell rattled when I leaned on it. The previous owners had ripped out the basement's wet bar when they moved, leaving random, exposed water pipes emerging from the floor. In the corner were hazy mirrors and liquor cabinets with plywood sliding doors. My mother threw an old yellow shag carpet over the cracked linoleum tiles, my father built shelves for our games, and the basement became our junk room, a place without restriction.

At night, the basement was creepy. My mother sent me downstairs for a spool of thread from her sewing machine, and I ran to escape the broad empty feeling that the room emitted. When my feet hit the floor tiles, a moist cold seeped into my bones. The yellow shag was some comfort, but tiny spiders lived in the piling. Along the windows sat doomed houseplants that my mother would not throw away until each leaf shriveled. The gangly philodendron and faded poinsettias sat on dim window ledges where they couldn't possibly recover. We called it the plant mortuary. When I consider it now, it's obvious my family couldn't address death and hardship openly, instead leaving them to wither in the corners. As a child, I felt their simple, carbon dioxide–depleted sighs.

In the daytime I loved that place. My sister, Marcy, and I left jigsaw puzzles on the floor until we'd done them all, and then we'd slide over their sleek surfaces (Monet, Big Bird, the Swiss Alps) in our sock feet. We built weeklong Lego castles. We could even roll up the carpet, strap on metal roller skates, and ride across the floor to the music of the Carpenters. The dress-up box was kept there, and we knelt to open it like the ark of the covenant. Inside we found my mother's prom dress, eggshell blue with two ruffled underskirts; my father's crazy, cast-off ties; cocky Irish caps, a pillbox hat, a beaded Indian headband I'd made in camp, a witch's hat left over from Halloween. . . . There were pairs of satin pumps, outrageous green and blue and red, which were incongruent with anything Marcy and I knew about adult women's wear. Our mother wore practical shoes, and she expected of us practical, straightforward lives. When we slid our feet into those high-heeled shoes, we became taller, more reckless and unstable than we otherwise might have dreamed. Down at the bottom of the chest were gaudy scarves, empty eyeglass frames, and costume jewelry. If we scrounged we could find safety pins to hold together the imaginary people we became.

It's important for me to remember the basement of my childhood because it resides underneath every other memory of home. Shelves of boxes contained my parents' past, mysterious and unmentioned. My father's workbench and mother's sewing table were the places I saw them most creative. And the satin pumps took Marcy, my best friend Linny, and me to new heights—we were handmaidens to a dying queen, sometimes played by my grandmother and sometimes by a large, red teddy bear my uncle won at an amusement park. When my grandmother took the role, she sat on a chair in the center of the room giving mild orders: "A cup of tea would be delightful just now." The queen was in better health when my grandmother was present. We curtseyed and catered to her make-believe whims. Today my grandmother is not well and perhaps better suited to the role. She remembers fondly the three of us spiraling around her, each of us bedecked in her daughter's old finery. My grandmother had sewn those dresses.

When the teddy bear filled in, our circumstances grew grim. She was a demanding matriarch, propped up in a chair, extracting from us not just our loyalty but our very life. It took courage to approach her throne. As Her Majesty ailed and foundered near death's door, the challenge of serving her grew severe. Our youth was a potion she drank in heaving gulps. After an audience, we teetered back to our safe corner to comfort one another. The queen wasn't especially evil; she ruled justly and provided for her servants. She just needed more than we were able to give.

Then we discovered a special power in the friendship between handmaidens. Linny knelt; I placed my hands on her bowed head. In an instant of silent concentration, I transferred all my strength into her body. Energy became a gift. Because of our boundless love for each other and our common devotion to the queen, we could give of our spirits the same way our parents donated blood at the Red Cross drive. Afterward, the giver was weak, curled on the carpet in a fetal tuck. The receiver stood taller than ever in her high heels. We called our drama "Spirit and a Half" because that's how much energy it took to serve the queen.

The story developed over two summer vacations when I was seven and eight, but one moment alone rises out of hundreds of basement hours. It was an unrelentingly muggy July. Even through the closed windows we could hear the continuous, high-pitched whine of the cicadas. The cracked tiles were cool against our feet. Linny clasped the cut-plastic diamond necklace behind her fine hair. It was her turn to wait on the queen.

Her Majesty was on her deathbed. She lay stiffly against the wall with her neckless head held at an improbable angle by the molding. There was little left for us to do except ease her way into the afterlife. In our dressing corner, Linny fell to her knees. I placed my hands on her thin, blond hair, took an expansive breath, and sent her all the energy I could muster. My brow was knit, my body strained. Linny's chin rested on her chest. Her face turned red and she suddenly began to weep.

I looked with compassion into Linny's tear-streaked face. When our eyes met, we felt a unity so compelling it made the rest of our childhood friendship seem common and unrealized. Then the spell broke. We burst into giggles and tripped in a mad rush up the stairs to tell my mother, "Look what happened! Linny cried!" My mother was peeling a carrot into the sink and stopped with the peeler poised at the fat end, about to be drawn forward. She turned to us, standing in the kitchen sunlight all got up in blue frills, heels, fake jewelry, and flushed with excitement. She smiled. Then she pulled the peeler toward her in a streak of orange.

Now I recognize how the basement invited us children to try on more than fancy dresses. Whole realms otherwise forbidden to us—sickness, death, royalty, intuitive powers, communal energy—we could *touch*, we could *live*. Without the unhindered freedom of a messy, private room and the time to unfold our story, we would never have had that stunning instance of connection that I now know to be the only mystical experience I've ever shared with another person. In the dark, the basement was threatening, its shadows concealing what we most feared, and in the light it invited us to potential so powerful we no longer recognized ourselves. We pulled dreams from the storage box labeled "unimaginable" into a place of likelihood; we tried them on; we felt what it meant to wobble about in their shoes. These lives were other than our own but perhaps more essentially our own than the school playground or piano lessons. If we could act out the life of castle troubadours, then our bodies contained the possibility of poetry and we were one step nearer to walking with those poems up the stairs, to the place where our desires had consequence.

During my house-hunting days (or, more accurately, house-clarifying days; with every front door my realtor unlocked, my affinity for Frank's house intensified), I nosed through closets and examined furnaces, aware that this was my opportunity to pick a metaphor. The architecture of a house would determine how many guests I could invite for dinner and the number of hangers I could use at once and how many books I could own and whether I could walk around naked. It would frame with a window some view that then would appear in my writing. What frame, what view, would work for me? More importantly, the house would sink into my psyche, determining how much sunlight might enter and where I'd face the shadows. Needless to say, I wanted to choose wisely.

I paced the perimeter of Frank's basement, wondering whether it was feasible to recreate what I took for granted growing up—room for the imagination at the foundation of things. The electrical box hummed in the corner; the laundry chute was a hole spilling darkness. Shiny tubing caterpillared from the dryer through the wall. The coal room's wainscot walls, extending out from the cement blocks, were dirty white. I considered Frank's ghost, her inclinations for cobwebs and terrorizing cats. I didn't and still cannot put much stock in souls getting caught between life and whatever comes next. Or at least I don't believe that souls take a form separate from those whose lives they've touched. But I trusted Frank enough to trust his experience of the ghost. Perhaps she served a purpose equivalent to the ornery queen of my childhood, helping Frank to face squarely what otherwise might haunt him from behind. I had too much respect for imagination to dismiss Frank's ghost as "just fantasy."

Although I didn't outright believe in Frank's ghost, she charmed me into loving his basement above all the others. If this space could allow her skulking, hypothetical presence, surely whatever ghosts I conjured up could live here as well. What mattered was that, at the foundation of home, there resides a place of ultimate permission.

One Sunday during that time, my congregation sang, "The church's one foundation is Jesus Christ her Lord." I laughed aloud. By then I was obsessed with basements, and here they appeared again, lurking in the theology of my faith. The source of our existence, the ground of our being, that which supports and sustains us we call *God* and sing its praises with unthinking gusto. I've yet to find a church that doesn't keep a baby Jesus, perhaps missing an arm, sound asleep among the storage boxes in the basement. So instead of listening to the sermon, I considered what, exactly, composes our "one foundation."

I was raised in a United Methodist Church founded in 1796; the brick building we worshiped in had been around since 1837. It was a simple, square structure without a steeple, with plain stained-glass windows tapering up broad walls. The sanctuary was intriguing for its high ceiling and half-moon altar in a draped alcove. Behind the sanctuary were the former fellowship halls, spacious rooms converted to dance studios and rented out to help pay the upkeep, and the kitchen, a practical room that had been renovated in the 1920s. The stove had twelve burners and three separate ovens that singed the facial hair of whichever trustee lit the pilot. In the center of the kitchen sat a mammoth butcher-block table, where potluck casseroles were garnished and brownies sliced.

For all the vast building on that property, it now seems strange to me that there were only two small basements—one under the kitchen, the other beneath the near half of the sanctuary. As children we weren't allowed in the kitchen basement because the stairs were steep and rotting. Only once did my father escort us down there to show us the dirt floor, stone walls, and two tenpin alleys stretching the back width of the building. During the heyday of our congregation, the youth sat along the painted, wooden benches drinking lemonade and hitting strikes. The pins and heavy balls still rested in a metal cabinet under decades of dust. After that, every time I found the door open I hovered at the top of the stairs. The basement contained lively memories that I, growing up as our congregation aged and faltered, could barely envision.

Underneath the sanctuary, half the basement was finished with Sunday school rooms whose carpeting smelled moldy. The other half, located behind a cheap plywood door, was a windowless storage room with rough-hewn planks for floorboards. Cabinets of Bible coloring books, faded construction paper, and the stubby ends of pew pencils were kept there. This basement was fair game for us kids. With two or three bare lightbulbs pushing darkness into the corners, we discovered stacks of pews, boxes, velvet-upholstered furniture, books, all in disorderly piles along the walls and in the center of the room. Once we pulled out a wooden highchair with a puzzling set of wheels at the rear base of the seat. In the light we found a lock and hinge; we bent the top half forward and, miracle of miracles, converted the highchair into a go-cart! Our treasure wasn't buried in a field; it was *right here*.

One summer, in preparation for a church auction, the trustees finally organized that disastrous basement. At the back of one heap of boxes they uncovered a wooden crate, two-by-eight feet, leaned up against the wall. They pried it open to find a stained glass window portraying Anna Howard Shaw. No one had heard of her. After some research we learned that in 1880, Anna was the first woman ordained in the Methodist Church; the controversial ordination was held in Tarrytown, and the window made to commemorate the event. Anna became a fire-and-brimstone preacher, itinerant in true Methodist tradition, sharp and determined. On one long carriage ride from the train station to a meeting, the driver stopped the horses and told Anna that women weren't meant to serve the Lord; they were meant for other purposes, which he proceeded to press upon her. But she had come prepared and held a pistol to his head for the remainder of the trip. The trustees donated the window to Boston Theological Seminary, where she had been one of two lonely women attending classes. The seminary hung it on a library landing where, at one point, Anna had passed out from hunger. Male seminarians received free room and subsidized board. As a woman, Anna was given two dollars a week.

On top of the church substructure we went about the weekly routine of worship. We were Methodists of a mild and proper variety, paying respects to a middle-class God, a historical Jesus, and a Spirit who was polite enough to remain within the confines of Bible stories. Just as Jesus foretold, the Holy Ghost inflamed the apostles, burning blue above their brows and speaking through them in tongues, but—thank heavens—never leapt past the bouncy typeface and bland language of our Good News Bible. We were beyond such insanity.

From the pulpit, Spirit was made flesh in an intellectual and Protestant way: it became the Word that we read two millennia later. Sun slanted through colored glass and landed in odd places (Mr. Whitney's bald head, for instance) as the pastor whined about the world. "'Then the devil left him,'" he read during a service for graduating seniors. The text was Jesus' temptation in the wilderness. "'And behold, angels came and ministered to him.'" He paused for dramatic effect. "You are entering a wilderness now—the wilderness of college and the workforce, where alcohol and money and other temptations will lure you from the path of what is right." We seniors stared ahead blankly, as though these temptations were unfamiliar. We scratched our polyester gowns. "But God will send angels to accompany you. Not anything supernatural," he clarified. "The ordinary people around you will uphold you."

No one believed in literal angels. Angels, the Son of God, and a meddling Holy Ghost may have existed in the past, but now they were figurative characters in our heady world. They resided within stories that, unlike the ghost stories we kids told one another during overnight lock-ins, the context of religion lent gravity and import. We were not to believe these stories, but to believe *in* them. "For truly, I say to you, if you have faith as a grain of mustard seed, you will say to this mountain, 'Move from here to there,' and it will move; and nothing will be impossible for you." Yet many things were. Words instructing us in what wasn't possible were strung across the sanctuary's expanse like yellow police tape. In confirmation class I learned that Jesus taught about the mustard seed in Biblical Times, a mystical era when everyone wore sandals and energy could flow from a man's cloak into the woman who touched it. We in twentieth-century America were different. No amount of faith would transport those blue, lounging hills just up the Hudson. Science explained land movement; medicine made people well. It never occurred to us that the Bible might describe, albeit extravagantly, a real experience of Spirit still available to humanity.

Looking back, it seems some essential link was missing in our faith. Perhaps the route between the basements (where objects were more than they appeared, where liberating secrets—a woman in our pulpit!—were made manifest) and our sanctuary was too circuitous; the door to the kitchen cellar was usually locked; two curved staircases and three rooms separated the Sunday school basement from worship. A direct encounter with the sacred was available to Jesus but not to us. Our minds could not encompass the honest possibility—the flesh-and-bones like-lihood—of Spirit appearing as we sang our raucous hymns or shook one another's hands. As a result, we missed the continuity that Christianity might have provided, that story, fictive or scriptural or otherwise, can describe truths that don't diminish with age. Sunday after Sunday, we dismissed our marvelous foundation and instead milled around in the light, where there were no ghosts, where what was on the surface was what was real.

Like anything built from the ground up, faith has an architecture: a basement, rooms, and roof beams. Some things about God we learn when the pastor visits; she perches on the couch's edge and asks after the state of our soul. But mostly the Spirit seeps into our bodies like the moist chill of a basement floor on bare feet. We walk about the house, our house, a house of prayer, and breathe in its open spaces and shadowed corners. It seems like just a house, when in fact it's a framework for residing in the world. Our questions and answers all begin with cement and end with roof tiles. Or they begin beneath, in the dark dirt, and end with smoke rising skyward from our chimneys. In other words, faith is a container. Its walls shape the spirit inside.

The church I attend now—only a hundred years old—has an alluringly stocky basement. You can still see shovel marks against the back bulwark. Two fifty-gallon surge tanks hang from the ceiling, the boiler squats ignobly in the room's center, and plumbing untangles itself as it travels upward into office and sanctuary. Of course this is Minnesota, so the trustees are unconscionably tidy. The minimal clutter can't be helped—snow shovels, vacuum cleaners, a manger, and a few camels. A dozen angel wings reside in a box. Sometimes, when worship grows dull, I think about their gauzy flight.

I'm not particularly in favor of doctrine or creed, ordination, the elevation of holy texts, the institution of church, or, for that matter, Christianity. Like most religions, it has irreconcilable shortcomings and an unforgivable history. What I do favor is the attempt to make sense of things by living within a story. The Christian story, for good or ill, is my inheritance. Every Christmas, the children don angel wings and shepherd robes; little Mary rides the donkey back of some poor Sunday school teacher, and a baby doll is born! The teenagers tell it differently. No one believes Mary's teen pregnancy isn't the result of sleeping around. Her boyfriend ditches her. Mary walks the city streets looking for a homeless shelter with a spare bed. Jesus turns out to be a baby girl. When it comes to dwelling within a story, the adults are far more reticent, although we have our subtle, socially acceptable means—costumes, the pastor's white robe and the choir's slippery blue with triangle bibs; poetry, the sacred language of psalms and psalters, undulating recitations blending our voices; and ritual, breaking bread and passing the cup, allowing us to relive a moment that may or may not have happened but becomes true when we fall to our knees.

When I was a child taking Communion, I'd close my eyes so there'd be no distinction between that moment in the Upper Room and *now*. United Methodists ration the elements to one Sunday a month (more often, I suppose, would be too much holiness to bear). In deference to recovering alcoholics and our prohibitionary history, we use grape juice rather than wine. And, when I was growing up, for the sake of the person responsible for cleaning the Communion linens (my mother), we used white grape juice. The wine was watered down, but the bread was good—round, with a tough, yeasty crust. Implicitly I understood that we pretended to eat Christ's body and drink his blood, unlike the Catholics who believed they weren't pretending. We came as close to *belief* as *make believe*, but there drew the line.

Years later, in Minnesota, I shared the Eucharist for the first time with a small circle of Lutherans. When I raised the chalice to my lips and took a gulp, I nearly choked. It was wine; it burned my tongue and hit my throat with a jolt that grape juice never musters. My eyes stung with surprise. For a moment, time and memory fused. Communion wine was indeed the blood of Christ, just as the Catholics had purported. The ritual became the *real thing*. Here was life. Here was eternity.

There's a difference between believing a story and experiencing it. Even as a child I knew this. It takes some effort, but it's possible to walk into the realm of a narrative and live it, so that when the story exercises, you build up muscles, and when the story includes loss, your grief is real. The two places story brought me to my knees as a child were the Tarrytown basement and the Communion rail. The difference was that in church it was no longer child's play; it was religion, the way adults made sense of the world. Church was and still is one of the few places communities confront life's big questions. What is our origin? What happens when we die? What difference does love make, or hate, or the seemingly endless passage of time? Here we strain to lend life context and meaning; here we tentatively probe the darkness. Sometimes we get confused and worship the container (the tradition, the doctrine, the church) instead of what we hope it contains. When any religion insists that you believe its story at the expense of your own, its ritual becomes confining and the place of worship oppressive. Too often we ward off wonder more than welcome it.

Even bland Methodist ritual can fuse mystery to ordinary elements, to bread and grape juice or to heat rising from the furnace through the iron grates. The capacity to imagine puts us in relationship with mystery, which is our truest experience of God's nature. When I was a child, church stories helped mystery inhabit my bones and breath. At night, lying in bed, I pondered Mary. The Holy Ghost had impregnated her out of the blue; what if one day I woke up with God's child inside my belly? The prospect thrilled and horrified me. I imagined embryonic movements growing in unfathomable regions. There were recesses within my body I knew nothing about, as unnamed and unacknowledged as the three-quarters of the church with no basement. Late into the night I rehearsed explanations to teachers and friends in case new life should swell within me. Perhaps this same churning light at her center was what pulled Anna Howard Shaw forward through the threatening woods toward her call. Perhaps each body is a building that the Holy Ghost haunts until one day we wake up, writhing in pain and then holding a brilliant Christ child in our arms.

A few weeks before Frank and I closed on the house, his cat, Bailey, fell sick. She was sixteen and scrawny; Frank was already worried about how she'd weather the drive to Arizona. The vet recommended putting her to sleep. Bailey was curled in Frank's lap for her final moments. She lay her whiskered chin on his thigh. In the instant her breath passed out from her, Frank felt the ghost from his house in the clinic room—a movement, an accompanying. Then his beloved cat was dead. When he returned home, grief-stricken, the house was empty. He never sensed the ghost again.

I was both disappointed and relieved. Frank and I signed the papers; he handed me the key and shook my hand. On the first of July I unlocked the front door and entered my house. It was bare of any furniture, decorations, or dust. My footsteps echoed. The rooms were bright with summer, the windows open to the sultry air. Walking through this, my first house, I remembered reading about the Pueblo people, and how they understand shelter to be an extension of the natural and sacred realms. Later I found the passage, from Tessie Naranjo: "Houses are . . . symbols of the larger ordering of the universe in which mountains, hills, and valleys define spaces where humans can dwell. Building and creating shelter brings the human and cosmic forms together. The roof or ceiling of the structure may be seen as the sky, or the father, which protects and nurtures the people who live inside. The floor is the Mother Earth, which embraces us when we die." I descended the stairs to the basement, where my house's foundation is embraced by Mother Earth. With Frank's possessions gone, the basement was empty, and with the ghost purportedly gone, I found myself wondering how human and cosmic might come together now that I was dwelling here. What would become my ghost? In what ways would this house comfort me with familiarity, and how might it thrust me into the unknown?

The basements of the churches I've loved reveal the foundation of the spiritual life to be not belief so much as engagement with the mystery lurking at the base of all things. We build a framework on top of mystery because we need someplace to live, some manner of surviving nature's fury and our mundane, daily needs. The structures that support our growth and exploration and insight are the ones that encompass the known as well as unknown. I was fortunate that the faith of my upbringing included both the unexpected in gloomy basements and the inexplicable in twists of narrative; without these I might today be confined to a static, stifled doctrine of unyielding answers and a self-righteous God. Or I might have rejected faith entirely for the clarity of science, with its propensity to trust explanations. But even Albert Einstein felt imagination to be more valuable than knowledge. Whatever framework we choose to make our home, room for the imagination is what allows us to reach forward into possibility. The unknown keeps us lively, growing, and in love. That first day I reached overhead to touch the crossbeam spanning the length of the basement, sturdily supporting the floor of my new home. It was trustworthy. Overhead, my future vaulted forward.

Squirrels All Over the Place

MY NEIGHBOR EVELYN looks out her kitchen window into the branches of her maple and sees, balanced on a limb, a fat cherry tomato. When she phones me to describe it, a delighted hoot escapes me before I realize that, to Evelyn, this isn't a laughing matter. Like the perfect yellow bell pepper that had been chewed and strewn across her impeccable lawn a week prior, like the mulberries that had fallen on her side of the fence which she gathered meticulously and handed me in a plastic baggy, the tomato came from *my* garden and therefore, according to some Scandinavian-Minnesotan dictum, is my responsibility. I try to ease my breach of etiquette by wondering aloud whether the squirrel wanted the tomato to ripen a bit first. Evelyn's responding titter is polite and humorless.

Early in the spring Evelyn had new sod laid in her backyard, and she has spent the entire summer, as far as I can tell, chasing off squirrels. "Git!" she shouts, and claps sharply at them. "You know," she shares with me confidentially, "the squirrels climb your mulberry and get onto our roofs!" I nod as though I understand her implications. Chop down the mulberry? BB-gun the squirrels? When Evelyn isn't home, I watch the squirrels root and dig unhindered in her perfect grass, as is their instinct. I, of course, don't have this problem because my lawn is root bound and mostly weeds. In the front, where Evelyn's chemically treated sod confronts my patchy crabgrass and creeping charlie, there's no need for a fence to define the property line. Once I found Evelyn on her bad, retired knees uprooting dandelions that had illegally emigrated, and got my first taste of guilt in proper proportion to Evelyn's controlled cheeriness. For the following three weeks I spent evenings cross-legged on the lawn, digging out pointy roots along a two-foot margin. Later, the rest of my yard exploded with flying silver seeds. When the wind breathed southward, I watched these wispy angels glide over to my neighbor's pristine property, and I winced.

When the squirrels ran off with my prize-winning pepper, I wasn't pleased. I'll even admit to downright anger when I found my daffodil bulbs kicked up; hope for that burst of earthbound sunshine sustains me through the winter, and the squirrels' callous, pointless burrowing made mockery of my faith in nature. Still, I figure I'm sharing this little plot of land and must make certain compromises. The squirrels, with their twitchy scolding and frantic drag races around the tree trunks, are my neighbors. They are a given, part and parcel with the landscape. I accept their furry foibles with a human's deferential patience for animal life and a certain superior indifference in the face of Evelyn's frustration. Live with 'em and learn to love 'em, I want to tell her.

Despite months of harassment, the squirrels remain undaunted by Evelyn's reprimands. As soon as her backdoor slams, they're at it again, plundering the rich soil for their invisible, treasured nuts. I wonder when Evelyn will give up and welcome scampering wilderness into her perfect yard. The squirrels aren't going anywhere. Then again, neither is Evelyn. When will I no longer bristle at the digging of Evelyn's critical eye?

Moving In

I WOULD NEVER HAVE CHOSEN MINNESOTA, but here I am, perched on the plains, my tiny house overshadowed by a glinting city that sprouts, metallic and engineered, amid vast expanses of corn and soybeans. This is a region of prairie land (although little prairie remains) and glacial lakes—thousands, spotting the north woods and spreading thin in the southern counties. We throw our arm over the vast shoulder of Lake Superior, mother of all lakes, and we squeeze the Mississippi's first trickle from Lake Itasca. The headwaters are not much to look at, a wetland of wild rice spilling into a clear creek. The river turns north and then veers back, twisting surreptitiously through the Twin Cities and panning out into a valley that is worth visiting for its sudden bluffs and abundance of bald eagles. Most of the state is plain, level, understated. It's not a landscape that gets my blood pumping.

But place comes to me unbidden, like a vocation. Now these flat city streets are my streets; now this shimmering snake curved between Minneapolis and St. Paul (meandering, sluggish, without clear direction) is my river; now this huge, unyielding sky is my overhead heaven, and I belong here; I want to appreciate the graces of this land. I arrived in Minnesota the way each of us arrives in a family, inheriting its secrets, skin blemishes, and crazy uncles. When I was eighteen, looking at colleges from the insane competition of the East Coast, Minnesota was an easy rebellion. Fifteen years later I wake up here, aware suddenly of the thin-line sunsets and eternally straight highways—aware of my matchbox neighborhood, two-dimensional yard, and windows spying on unadorned houses in every direction—and wonder why this place holds me so strongly in its grip. If I choose not to leave this unimpassioned landscape, at least I can recognize its gifts.

I spend hours, days even, walking around city lakes. Each is encircled by paved paths for walking and biking, then by a street, then by the tony homes of the city's rich and established. Calhoun, Harriet, Lake of the Isles, Nokomis . . . I walk with my face toward the lake's surface, waiting for the landscape to exhilarate me. Most Minnesota lakes have no inlet or outlet and no internal spring; they are the remainders of glaciers melted into low-lying earth, and they make me restless. Self-contained and still as the fields at the city's margins, they lap lackadaisically, the wind spinning patterns on their surface, and are unconcerned with my bursting frustration. Water, the Hudson River taught me during my formative years, is meant to travel. The lakes have a different message. *This is where you are*, they say. *No need to move*.

Horizontal beauty, I decide, is subtle. Here the northern lights fill the broad night canvas; here coneflower, bluestem, and milkweed invite the monarch's fibrous affection; here the soil is as black as our dreams. In my garden I turn it over and find earthworms of nightmarish proportions, but this is a good sign— I'm on fertile ground. Ten blocks from my house I can sneak down into the Mississippi gorge, which tucks itself modestly below street level. The water moves, but at a muddy pace that's hardly noticeable. Instead I watch the swallows, the ravens clustered in burr oaks, the grapevines twining into any sunlit gap. In the sandstone cliffs I note eroded pockets and streaks. *Attend to the small*, I tell myself. *The minute is pleasing too.*

But the minute does not sweep me off my feet.

Every time I make some tentative peace with the prairie, my family visits. And I think of my father, standing before the living room windows in Tarrytown, New York, after our first family vacation in Europe, having seen the Thames, the Seine, the Rhine, the Danube; he swept his arms wide to encompass the grand, estuarial expanse—the mile-and-a-half width, the whitecaps, the barges and military vessels and occasional tall ships—and proclaimed the Hudson the most spectacular river in the world. It is. My parents fly in from the Hudson Valley, or my sister flies in from the high desert of Taos, New Mexico, where peaks pierce an unblinking sky; I pick them up at the airport and, driving into Minneapolis, see my landscape again through their eyes: understated, without flair or focus. The Minnesota River is at the right but you'd never know it, submerged as it is within its green floodplain beneath the highway. Our visits play themselves out over a backdrop of boredom. I take them to the theater, to our May Day Parade or the St. Paul Winter Carnival, in hopes of distracting them from the landscape. Once I took my sister canoeing down the St. Croix; we pulled out of the rapids to eat lunch and sat on the sand beside a hole the size of a quarter. Over the next hour, eighteen infant snapping turtles hatched, pulled themselves through the opening, and, after deliberation and much eye rubbing, trundled down to the river—with the exception of one, who determinedly marched uphill until we set it straight. After that, Marcy's appreciation for my state went up a notch. I could tempt her with a canoe trip in the Boundary Waters.

It's the people, I tell my family, who keep me here—my liberal congregation, a lively community of writers, a plethora of progressive theologians and organizations supporting the spiritual life, this neighborhood where strangers meeting on the sidewalk entertain lively debates about air temperature. The people don't differ much from the landscape. They are mild-mannered, practical, and hospitable, qualities that, for some reason, are more appealing in humans. Minnesotans keep the thermostat down and vote in primary elections. They are masters at holding strident opinions while avoiding conflict. My brassy, New York decisiveness meets with intimidated eyes and secret disdain. And my choices to be forthright about my bisexuality, to ditch the nine-to-five world of responsible work for a freelance career, and to periodically mention mystical experiences in casual conversation win me friends only along the margins. Fortunately, the margins are wide in the Twin Cities, due to Minnesota's heritage of public service and community activism. I've eased into this culture, my stride slowing considerably and my o's elongating into the Scandinavian cadence as though it's been waiting, dormant inside me.

Minnesota's seasons, at least, are strong-willed. By May, spring has unfurled its green enthusiasm; July's humidity and sweat are rivaled only by the mosquitoes they attract; the October colors are stunning, at least to a Dakotan or Nebraskan, and winter, of course, is lethal. Once, when a Seattle friend arrived at the Minneapolis airport in the middle of a blizzard, he got out to the curb, looked up, and said, "Ah, yes. You have weather here." The first time I experienced a tornado-green sky with its ensuing, capricious wind, I wanted to thrash about in a frenzied dance. I relish the extremes, the earth's severe tilt and our consequent thickening skin. If the land is a stage for the weather, perhaps that's enough to satisfy.

At a certain angle from my couch, an ash tree across the street fills my windows with its thick, arching limbs. This pleases me. I have a view, such as it is; I can let the tree's symmetry cross the sky and ease my ache for beauty. Place is a calling, a challenge to reconcile one's sense of home with what one is given. This house is so simple, so perfectly matched to the landscape. I relish Frank's whimsy with house paint (the claw-foot tub's toenails have red polish), as though these plumb walls and practical woodwork are an empty canvas. I take similar liberties in the yard. His rectangular, straight-rowed garden quickly acquired curved edges, and I've brought in soil to give it some dimension. By settling here, I'm accepting white stucco outside and smooth plaster inside; I'm agreeing to the lakes and their patient surfaces and the empty enormity of cornfields. What altitude, drama, and movement my setting lacks, it makes space for on the internal landscape. Aesthetic adventure and creative awe are relinquished to the ethereal regions of the heart.

And so I've moved in; I take a paintbrush to the front porch wall, I plant chamomile, butterfly weed, and native grasses, I attend our block party where I enthusiastically socialize with the neighbors, I plaster the refrigerator door with poetry and photographs, I arrange and rearrange the furniture to the sunlight's best advantage. My writing desk I position before the one window that peers across the street and between two houses, where sumac flares in the fall and a crabapple, tangled among scrub trees, distinguishes itself in May. When my need for a compelling landscape ripens, I sit here; I traverse the interior, where doubt moves in tectonic shifts, where imagination swells into an unhindered storm, where memory catches each splinter of light and prayer opens onto the billowing expanse.

Slave to Joy

I'M TOTING MY GROCERIES up the front steps when Chrissy, the red-haired eight-year-old twin from up the street, marches down the sidewalk and accosts me. She has her fingers in one of those paper fortune-telling contraptions kids make, with four pointed tips that flip back and forth and look like a bird's beak. Chrissy had colored the quadrants in dark magic marker—navy, rust red, green, and a purple that was running dry. "Will you play my game?" Chrissy asks.

I shift the grocery bag onto my hip. "Sure," I say.

I choose purple.

It takes Chrissy a few tries, but she spells out "P-U-R-P-L-E" and exposes the numbers on the inside for me to choose.

"Five," I select randomly. "F-I-V-E," Chrissy works her fingers back and forth, strangely spelling instead of counting. I choose the number six, and she lifts the paper flap to grant me my fortune.

"You will be a slave for the rest of your life!" Chrissy pronounces. This is the same kid who tried to set me up with her divorced father the week I moved onto the block.

"A slave!" I say, surprised. "Isn't that kind of harsh?"

Chrissy shrugs. It isn't her fate.

"Can I be a slave to joy?" I ask.

"No!" Chrissy protests. It is, apparently, too easy an out. "You're going to be a slave to a servant." She looks pleased with herself.

I am determined not to let this budding doomsdayist cast a pall over my future. "How about a slave to my cat?" I suggest.

Chrissy giggles. She thinks for a moment, then nods. I open the front door, put down the groceries, and hold Rhia so Chrissy can give her a few affectionate pats. Rhia's an ornery cat with a reputation for lashing at strangers. In my arms, though, her tension softens and she'll permit unfamiliar hands to scratch behind her ears. Chrissy is delighted. Rhia even licks her stubby fingers. With evidence of my slavery to this temperamental servant confirmed, Chrissy suddenly says "Okay!" and lets the screen slam behind her. I watch her hop along the sidewalk, eager to snare the next unwitting neighbor into her fatalistic game, and I smile when she begins to whistle. I am, after all, a slave to her joy.

On Shining Rails

ᴇarly on a summer morning when the house is dim and I've barely surfaced from sleep, a train whistle, thin and wraithlike, passes over the city and enters my bedroom. A long double pitch followed by the rumble of metal on metal. Night has chilled the air. I wake, but only enough to vaguely travel the whistle's airborne route, from Hiawatha Avenue where trains grind across city streets and align their freight cars, mouths open, beneath grain elevators grumbling with corn, moving eastward twelve hundred miles, through Chicago and Pittsburgh and Erie, Pennsylvania, over New York's hilly countryside to Albany, where the sound suddenly veers south, down the commuter line into the Hudson River Valley. It rounds a curve, sweeping the swamp tassels in a swift spiral. Then the echoing tones rise from the tracks, up a half acre of wooded lawn to the wide windows of my childhood home.

In the daytime, metro trains ran (and still run) every hour to and from New York City, more frequently during peak times.

First we'd hear a metallic twang like an aluminum sheet simulating a thunderstorm, then a held breath, and finally the seven-car commuter train burst around the corner, interrupting conversation and shaking the windows. To this day, when I speak with my parents over the phone in the summer, we pause midsentence to let the train pass, as though it's natural for New York commuters to render me speechless in my Minnesota home. During the night, freight trains trudged north to Albany carrying new cars from the GM plant in Tarrytown or overseas imports loaded from barges in New York harbor. My sister and I peered out the living room window, over yard and swamp, delighted when the heavy wheels kicked sparks: fireworks in the foreground, the Hudson's murky expanse, and, on the other shore, a few winking lights from the outskirts of Nyack. If the conductor blew the whistle at stray deer or fishermen, the sound passed up and down the valley, rebounding, carried by the water. No melody is more familiar to me. Train whistles wrap me in a mournful lullaby: "I'm not with you, but you're not alone."

It's strange to love a lumbering locomotive, with its graffitied boxcars and greasy engine. Every time I drive west from my Minneapolis home and get stuck in a line of traffic, waiting in front of flashing lights while engines maneuver boxcars in and out of warehouses, I wonder why I have patience for these unwieldy locomotives and not for the city buses, stopping at every other corner, or for planes whose shadows pass over us like portents of death. I don't usually feel affection toward vehicles of industry. The rails run north-south through a corridor of grain elevators—ungainly, towering cylinders prone to gang tags and the dark smudge of automobile exhaust. The air is yeasty there and, on humid summer days, sickly sweet. On either side of the road are orphaned boxcars. Further south, the rail peters out and has been ripped up to beautify a city park; a once-charming, boarded-up station sits beyond the last metal glint in the weeds.

Going north, the rails interrupt traffic for another two miles, then swing east, mysteriously slipping into the lesser-known arteries of the city. They reappear once over the interstate and once in a tough neighborhood where a friend of mine lives, where in late summer there's an abundance of wild sunflowers. Then I lose track.

Something about a train's whistle lifts my heart from my slumbering body; it pulls me outside of myself, across the city and along the silver lines that crisscross our country, joining urban sprawl to farming town and passing over hundreds of uninhabited miles. The strangers who grow our food, the hobos whose homes are always moving, the conductors leaning forward, the passengers facing the landscape, and me, lying heavy in bed—all are joined by a haunting, steam-driven sound. A pattern rises from this vast network of transportation, stirring me. How is it that we're connected? I want to know what binds people to one another, to the earth and to what's holy. Certain questions reside in every spiritual journey, and this one rumbles and shines.

Every autumn I attend a silent retreat on the north shore of Lake Superior. The spiritual director who is our host posts on her kitchen wall an elaboration on the word *namaste*, the East Indian greeting loosely interpreted to mean, "The god in me honors the god in you":

> I honor the place in you where the entire universe resides.
> I honor the place in you of love, of light, of truth, of peace.
> I honor the place within you where, if you are in that place in you and I am in that place in me, there is only one of us.

Following the moment I first read this, seven days of silence and the cold expanse of Lake Superior opened me wide. Only once, in the late evening, did I see the green starboard lights of a passing ship. I've understood the great longing of my life to be to return to the womb, where there is only one of us—surrounded and upheld, umbilical cord binding with flesh my body to the source of existence. Surely the warm place from which we enter the world is a foretaste of the inconceivable home to which we're going. With every spiritual growth spurt, I know a bit more clearly that womb "of love, of light, of truth, of peace." And I'm a bit more confounded. We are already there, connected to the source of love. How come, then, on most days I can't feel it?

I ride the rails. Steel on steel is a speeding heartbeat. Outside all is motion; inside it is still except the rocking in our hips. A woman's head bounces lightly against the window. A man hums under his breath, matching the pitch to the drone below us. On this kind of journey, there's not much to do other than watch the landscape, foreground an impressionistic blur of cattails, marsh grass, and radiant purple loose strife; the horizon, steady corn-fields, one rolling over the next. A horse, a collapsed silo, a dirt road with a car driving parallel and losing ground, trailing its wake of dust. On the surface of things, I'm traveling from one place to the next across a distance, measuring miles by the intake and release of breath. When the train stops, I'll emerge in another state. For now, I stand in the aisle and jump, the way I did as a child; I land back a few centimeters from where I started. Left to its own devices, the body prefers the familiar turf of the past. I'm covering ground, and at the same time my leaps for answers move me back in time, not toward solutions but to the source of my question.

When I was young—when I used to lie in bed listening to the waves and the thundering freights and the pulsing chorus of peepers—I had strong passions and cast my longing into the night like a fine fishing line. For a long while I was in love with my English teacher, Mr. Polliche, but beyond writing letters I'd never send and getting perfect scores on every paper, what could a twelve-year-old do? Mr. Polliche taught us how a metaphor can pack an image with meaning, and he disclosed a secret I'd always suspected, that our lives are like poetry, layered and resonant. With hindsight I see that I confused metaphor with Mr. Polliche's brown eyes and heavy brows. It's easier to fall in love with a man than a concept, especially when you're in seventh grade. The night air breathed in, drawing the lace curtains tight against the screen, and then breathed out. I wasn't imagining it; Mr. Polliche and I *were* connected, if only by our love of literature and our mutual respect. In the darkness the connection seemed tangible, everyone's longing sent out as gossamer thread binding one to another in a fairy web, which morning light rendered invisible. I wondered if I might pluck the cords the way a spider does, creating a silent vibration. I wondered if, to another spider, it might sound like music.

The dark revealed these dreamy fibers and more. Occasionally in the spring a train kicked a spark into the hollow stalks of the previous year's swamp grass. Fire flared, rapidly spreading north and south along the raised rail bed and creeping east toward our house. My sister slept soundly through these nights. I awoke with the siren's decline as fire engines turned onto our street, and felt my heart race as red lights were thrown across the bedroom ceiling. Ours was the only house on the block with easy access to the swamp. To the north, the houses lined a bay of the river cut off by the railroad and tangled with grapevines. To the south the shoreline suddenly grew steep, so that houses perched on the rising edge of a cliff. Only at our house could the firemen drag hoses down the driveway and across the backyard, and send water arching over the twenty-foot bank into the swamp. I stood at the living room window, barefoot, in my nightgown, watching shadows of men lurch against the blaze. Once they had arrived, my parents assured me, there was little risk of fire climbing into the yard, although the previous owners had told us of an occasion when fire had lapped at the back patio, and I knew for a fact that there was an ancient, scorched apple tree just over the north edge of the yard. I had climbed it, and afterward washed black off my hands in the gutter runoff.

I loved it when the swamp burned. Ours was a suburban, commuting neighborhood where working couples owned large houses and raised few kids. We knew only a handful of people on the block and delivered my mother's kuchen to them on Christmas Eve—two cranky ladies and an elderly couple on either side of us, the neighbors in the brick colonial across the street and in a contemporary home with a skylight at the top of Pokahoe hill. But even these acquaintances we saw only twice or three times a year. On nights when men's shouts and the fire's roar woke the block, everyone turned out in nightshirts and bathrobes, congregating in huddles below me. I imagined them murmuring reassurances and recounting past fires, including the Easter eve when the railroad company sent a helicopter. My mother brought hot mugs of coffee out to the firemen and paused to shiver with the neighbors. My father watched by my side, vowing to donate more this year to the volunteer fire department.

The next morning, neighbors returned to look down at the blackened strip of earth and comment on how many trees burned, who made the initial phone call, and wasn't it a shame to lose the spring peepers? I stood among the adults feeling proud that our house was the center of excitement, while my sister pouted from the sidelines ("Wake me up next time," she whined). We weren't so separate from our neighbors after all; it only took a spark, just as the campfire song said. Fire was enough to draw us together, even though we didn't know each other's names. It was for this reason, and not my parents' gentle assurances, that I was never afraid. A scorched, sweet reed smell permeated the air. It wouldn't be long—a week at most—before a green flush covered the damp earth and the peepers' high-pitched pulse started up again.

God exists *between*; God is the binding, the breathing, the cast line and smoky thread. When I used to live in the woods and walked first thing in the morning, finely spun strands caught my face and trailed behind like streamers. I swiped at them, but a single-skeined web is more like a thought than a thing. It disappears before it can be tossed into the underbrush. What two parts of the dewy woods aren't connected in the morning? The rusting petals of trillium? Shelf fungi, leaking water from their undersides? A dying branch, a fox, a snake hole? In the woods, the carcass of a goldfinch cracked from its egg is just more humus for the bloodroot. Between rock and puddle, insect and moss, hawk and mouse is a generative tug. I may not be able to hold it, but I can feel it brush my cheek.

Meanwhile, in Australia a butterfly is flitting among the eucalyptus trees. The flap of its iridescent wings is cause for speculation: Is the hurricane forecast to pummel the eastern seaboard originally due to this small disturbance of air? Chaos theory says it's possible; there are patterns of order and beauty hidden within the seemingly random nature of the universe. The intricate ways we are connected, insect to storm, stone to star, human to human, are easier to discount than comprehend. Here in the Midwest, the monarchs' migration gets interrupted by an insect-resistant breed of corn. A field where they land for nourishment now provides nothing, and, as a result, less pollination occurs up in the north woods of Canada and down in the rain forests of Brazil. Orange and black wings litter paved roads across South Dakota. Which are the flowers that no longer bloom?

35

I'd rather overlook such subtle relations and see instead what is immediate and direct: how touching the woman I love transforms her. With my hand at her heart she sighs; on her belly her eyes widen. Connection ripens. Cause and effect are as clear as the pale curve of skin in her collarbone. When we touch each other deeply, it is literal, and moist.

What rises to the surface, flesh against flesh, is a minor incarnation of a greater connection. I'm less able to recognize it, but touch is only sometimes tactile. More often it runs its course beneath awareness: the random bump of shopping carts, the misheard whisper, the chance phrase leaping from a printed page, a stranger's wince. The prayer sent out in one lifetime and answered, without acknowledgment, in another. We touch one another gently, wantonly, painfully, invisibly; through walls, through layers of earth; across races, species, space, and time. But always there's touch. Isolation is a myth. It's easier to see what is simple, the pressure of my hand in another's, than to grasp that there's no hand mine does not touch. A butterfly stirs up the wind. Humanity exerts its irrevocable presence on the world.

Less than a year after I moved into my Minneapolis home, my neighbor to the north committed suicide. He was thirty-nine, a shy, gruff man who drove a tow truck and spent every spare minute, including his last, tinkering on junk cars in the garage. His brunette girlfriend was a nurse who visited at erratic hours. I had chatted with Jack perhaps a dozen times over the months. Once he and a friend took a sledge hammer to one of two misshapen cemented stone pillars in his yard, supposedly the remains of an archway into what used to be a churchyard. I went out after five hours of crashes and cursing to joke about homeowner projects we regret starting. They never tackled the second pillar. After my house was burglarized he leaned over the fence to say, "That sucks. This used to be a safe neighborhood." Once when I was reading the paper in the backyard, I put it down to say hello, which I don't always do. "Oh, hi," Jack said. "You're not mad at me for some reason?"

"Goodness no," I replied. "You mean because I'm not always friendly?"

He nodded. His awkwardness made me feel like a schoolkid.

"I'm used to more privacy than you get in the city," I said. "It has nothing to do with you."

"Oh, good." He was visibly relieved. I took a sip of lemonade and felt for the thousandth time surprise at my unthinking impact on others.

Most of what I knew about Jack I gathered from the close proximity of city living. His best friend—the only one who spoke at his funeral—came over on Saturday mornings in a baby blue Impala and entered Jack's backdoor with a twelve-pack of Cokes. When the weather was warm, some variety of beaten-up, broken-down car was usually parked in Jack's driveway. The owners (often women, sometimes bedraggled couples, none of whom I ever saw a second time) would lean against the garage and talk with Jack in low voices as he fiddled under the hood. For a period of two weeks in January, a woman's unfamiliar, drunken voice woke me up during the midnight hours by knocking loudly and shouting, "Open up, Jack! I know you're there." He never let her in. I wondered where she would go to sleep at that hour, in the below-zero weather.

I returned home late one Saturday night to find Jack's girlfriend doing CPR in the driveway between our houses. Kathleen had dragged Jack out of the garage, the screen door still propped open by his foot. When the medics arrived, I showed them to Jack, lying shirtless and breathless in the dirt. Soon it was clear there was nothing more they could do. The medics aired the exhaust out of the garage and left with the body. Later, Kathleen told me she'd done CPR innumerable times, but this was the first she'd done it on someone she loved. "It was hell," she said. Any signs of depression Jack had shown were private, not the sort of information a grieving girlfriend tells a neighbor.

With the exception of his friend's brief testimony, Jack's funeral was ghastly. The parlor's electric organ droned out tinny, irrelevant hymns. A hulking pastor read Jack's obituary, then launched into a sermon about another man who died young, who was our friend and savior. I looked around at the restless men in jeans and Harley T-shirts and the middle-aged women with too much makeup. When two different cell phones went off during the service, I watched their respective owners blush, and I wondered what (if any) comfort they found in this grisly, impersonal ritual. How could we make sense out of a self-conscious mechanic committing suicide? I felt Jack's absence acutely—an empty house next door—even though I hardly knew him. Perhaps no one knew him. Yet we all felt the tug to be with Jack one last time, in the only way we thought possible. I slipped out as soon as the service ended, passing between some smokers who had never made it into the chapel but instead huddled together, hunched and grim, whispering in the morning sunlight.

When people have relinquished the language of religion and are still seeking, still longing, they often talk about *feeling connected*. The words are paltry, but what they mean is that sense of touching the source of life in a raw way, without the rigmarole of dogma. Simone Weil called it "implicit faith"—our response to naked, sacred experience. Weil believed it easier for a non-Christian to become a Christian than for a "Christian" to become one. It's a paradox similar to the Zen koan, "If you meet the Buddha in the road, kill him." Sometimes religious traditions hinder the spiritual development of practitioners. It's not the trains that interest me so much, speeding from this place to the next hauling grain or steel or people, as it is the rails that shimmer beneath them. What kind of pattern has been laid across the curved acres of this earth, tying together humanity's remotest regions and making of us a whole? Can anything unite these disparate fragments, so we might find meaning even in death?

When I lived in the woods, the railroad ran from the Iron Range and Duluth past the small town of Grandy, which consists of a post office, an antique store, and a bar known for its broasted chicken. Our house was five gravel miles away, isolated by washboard-rutted roads and a dense stand of Norwegian pines. Country roads don't warrant flashing signals at railroad crossings, and so trains forewarned us by blowing their whistles. Within hearing of the house were three crossings: one north near Stanchfield, one where our road hit the highway, and one south of Grandy. Trains passed every few hours throughout the day, their sounds blending with daytime noises—the highway's faint hum, construction in the woods, crows, hawks ruefully circling, cicadas, a chain saw. . . . At night the train whistle flew miles over the flat, sleeping landscape. The metallic growling of boxcars came through the earth, quaking below us.

Each engineer has a distinct pattern of whistle blowing. I never noticed it until, in the middle of a conversation with the local baker, she turned eastward and said, "There goes Harry." After that, I lay in bed at night and kept track of who was conducting at what hour: long, long, short-long at eleven; short-long, short-long at three. The whistle was then more like a signature scrawled across the night. Loons do the same thing, calling at dusk with plaintive, primitive voices. Each diapason is distinct, then dissolves into darkness. Even when we don't know it, we cast the nets that connect us. Our individual shouts form a pattern: a constellation of sound.

The other day a friend told me about a rail yard in the bowels of St. Paul, a vast steel landscape bypassed by the city streets.

Apparently I've driven over it a dozen times. The bridge's walls are high; we're meant not to notice, and this intrigues me. In my imagination I go there at night, driving away from the tree-lined boulevards and the billboarded business district down a trucker's route with no name, past a tall chain-link fence into this wide, industrial field. Towering floodlights reveal acres of trains. Here is where the rails converge like hundreds of frozen streams at a confluence, or like digressive voices of a chorus suddenly consonant on a single chord. Parallels of silver span the earth. Under the harsh light the boxcars show their colors—rust and factory green, Soo Line, Santa Fe, Canada—but across most of the yard they are black, hulking tombs. The shadows of open boxcars harbor the homeless, perhaps, or hobos who choose this as home. Rats scamper after fallen grain. The ground here is gravel, ties, ragweed, and metal; it would be easy to move without making a sound. In some distant section there's the thunder and high-pitched screech of movement. Here, all is still. We are waiting—for a shipment, for an engine, for our turn, for the daylight. For our body to shift, beginning its slow climb into motion. On shining rails, heaviness transforms itself into speed. The night yard holds this secret.

When I lie naked under a blanket on the massage table, Bridget, my massage therapist, works the reflex points along my foot and heel, creating a momentary intense pain in my stomach and then a cramp in my arm. Bridget has lithe hands that are remarkably strong. She reads the sole of my foot as a map of internal organs, probing and pushing inner regions through the surface of skin. I don't often give much thought to these recesses of my body; it's a dense, whirling realm in there, full of quiet but vital activity. Bridget uses a technique called polarity, pressing one finger into my heel, the other into a small soft space in my hip, then holding them both for a period. Her pressure draws a line between two points that have never been touched simultaneously. Suddenly they seem eager to communicate. Or she'll join my hip to the center of my forehead, a crux of movement to the nexus of thought. Bridget traces meridians coursing the realm of my body. I imagine them like the song lines of Aboriginal Australia, paths that the ancestors sang into existence as they traversed the outback. How long have I lived in my body? Only today, for the first time, does the thick bone of my forehead sing to the swing-set socket of my hip.

Thoughts shift and link. We're less likely now to credit the brain with all thinking processes; memory, it's suspected, resides in individual cells and surfaces with a familiar smell or a massaged muscle. And where resides the soul? Here is a universe of spit and scalp, liver and vulva and tongue, palm, pigment, tears, cornea, toenail, bone marrow, breath. It is uncharted territory—we know what's here, but we don't understand how a dream wakes us in a cold sweat, or what the yogis mean by kundalini energy spiraling up their spines like an orgasmic snake. The pattern that unites the bending of my knees with my heart's sinking into quiet is not just about faith. It is organic; it's about biology. It's about touching those invisible lines of connection strung tight to give us each life and hung loose to wed us to the world.

Maybe our universe is a growing, breathing organism. Death, then, is a dry fleck of skin brushed off its brow, and birth is a toenail grown too long. Or birth is an insight that alters slightly how the eyes perceive. The edge of the universe is expanding at the speed of light, a phenomenal fact unless given in proportion; two light years of growth each year isn't much if you're already 40 billion light years wide. A star's pulse isn't a heartbeat; it's the flicker of an eyelash. A human is one electron, more or less. Given the scale of things, how on earth can we proceed?

We are specks of dust forming the whole. A childhood friend of mine once drew a horse by making the body out of hundreds of miniature horses. Look closely at the mane, the flaring nostrils, or the muscled flanks and you'd find minute, rearing stallions. At about the same time I discovered that the spin of atoms mirrored the twirling of planets (at age nine, surely I was the first to see it!). The symmetry still amazes me: Heaven's likeness residing inside us. Today physicists look at a hologram, any small piece of which reveals the entire image, and they see a model for understanding the universe. The whole is contained in each of its parts. The universe rears its head within my cells.

There's a Hasidic story about a Jew who walked through life carrying two verses from the Torah written on slips of paper, one in each jacket pocket. He referred to one and then the other throughout the day. In his left pocket the verse read, "Dust to dust." In his right pocket the verse read, "For you the universe was made." The paradox is acute and resplendent. "I am Nobody—who are you?" asks Emily Dickinson. "I am large, I contain multitudes," exudes Walt Whitman, and both are true. The slips of paper weigh down my pockets. I can only read one at a time.

No matter how tightly I press my body to another, I can't melt into her skin or crawl back into the womb. Flesh creates boundaries. Uniqueness separates us; personality pulls us apart. Day in and day out, this is the poignant ache that gnaws at me. Ultimately we are each alone. Even divinity is vastly separate—the Great Alone, the godhead, untouchable as the big bang's burst. At the same time, the dust of which we're composed is stardust, with its origin at the conception of time. There is no place where divinity is not; there are no two points between which a line isn't already drawn. We are infused with holiness, intimately bound to one another, to the earth and to eternity. When I despaired of doing the hard, inner work of fighting depression, a friend told me, "Your effort contributes to everyone's well-being." She saw what I couldn't: an infrastructure of veins coursing through the universal body. My state of mind, the smile I don't flash at a neighbor, the writing I send out in sealed manila envelopes, all travel by means I can't comprehend to a destination I can't imagine. The possibilities of connection are awful. Who can bear the responsibility? And who *wouldn't* want it?

At the end of November 1994, my sister Marcy gave birth to her first child at home in Taos, New Mexico. Simon was a sweet fellow with a pug nose and a whiff of auburn hair, who slept with his hands over his head the same way I do, the same as my mother and grandmother. Since the extended family had planned to gather at my parents' home for the holidays, we postponed meeting Simon until then. It wasn't easy; for the first time I had a nephew, gurgling at the other end of the telephone line, and I was eager to hold him. Then, four days before Christmas, between his 4:00 A.M. feeding and dawn, Simon mysteriously stopped breathing and died. There was nothing anyone could do. Marcy and I both moved our plane tickets up a few days and fled to New York. We held each other and cried, while in Albuquerque an autopsy was done and Simon was cremated.

 The day I remember most clearly was December 22. We were expecting Simon's ashes to be delivered midafternoon; that much of him, at least, we would have with us. My parents' pastor joined our family in the living room, where we sat numbly, unable to make a cup of tea or conversation. The sun, warm for December, reflected light off the Hudson onto the far wall. I sat beside the window looking out into the yard. Straight, wide shadows of tulip trees and hemlocks striped the lawn, still remarkably lush with even a few dandelions blooming. A male cardinal hopped along the margin of a shadow. When my maternal grandfather died, a cardinal frequented the lilac bush outside my grandmother's kitchen window. Day after day, in the midst of her grief, she stood at the sink doing dishes and suddenly this shocking bird would appear, scolding with his sharp chip-chip. At first it was a brief distraction from sorrow, but, after months, it became a burst of joy—a visit from the dead, she said; Gramps come back to keep her company. She began collecting cardinals—on tea towels, on her outdoor thermometer—as a reminder of how near the dead reside. I watched the scarlet flash for a good quarter hour before I pointed it out to my sister.

She stood and came to the window. "Look," I said. It pecked the ground, first in then out of the light. Its red crown bobbed at us.

"Oh!" she said.

The doorbell rang; a delivery man handed my sister a small cardboard box. Inside was a metal cube four inches square. Simon's ashes were lighter than breath.

My father and I couldn't bear to sit anymore. We left the family in the living room and did something we'd never done before, something he and my mother had forbidden while I was growing up: We crossed the lawn, skidded down the steep slope to the swamp, bushwhacked our way between the tall, dry grasses and climbed up to the railroad bed. Gravel slipped from under our feet until we reached the rails, warm and humming. By this time the sun was low in the southern sky, angling up the river with surprising intensity. We walked the tracks together, silent. To our left stretched the two-mile breadth of the Hudson, and to our right, once we'd passed our neighbor's house, was swamp and a tangle of dead grape vines, bare oaks, dusty-green hemlocks, and sections of mangled chain-link fence. The air was crisp but pungent with sea salt. When we came to an abandoned stone boathouse built by the Rockefellers, we gingerly stepped over the active third rails in order to peer inside. The stones were cold, layered with the Hudson's thick green algae. Everything was touched by the sun's sideways gold. When a train passed, its roar shook every cell in my body. I ached so badly that I didn't want to stop walking, foot in front of foot from one railway tie to the next, past Ossining and Croton and Kingston and Albany, north into the Adirondack mountains with the river narrowing beside me until I'd arrive at Tear in the Clouds, the Hudson's headwaters, a still lake into which, perhaps, down near the cold spring that feeds it, sorrow sinks into eternity. The dead flash their scarlet wings there; the living turn their faces toward the sun. Surely, in places, heaven is without boundaries, its bright dissolution not entirely outside our reach.

My father and I walked until the sun brushed the palisades, and then we turned our backs to the river, crossed the tracks, and climbed a fence into the woods. The paths there were dark and meandering. We both felt chilled; it was December, after all. When he was in his mid-thirties, my father walked to and from his office on those paths. Now I imagined him as a young man swinging his briefcase, hoping his two daughters would race up to meet him under this mesh of branches. Occasionally we did, braving those first few minutes in the woods without him for the sake of then holding his hand. Oaks towered overhead; hemlocks dropped their soft cones, and moist, gray leaves layered the path. By the time we emerged onto the street a few blocks from home, dusk had fallen. Lamps burned yellow inside the houses and our footsteps echoed off the pavement. I no longer recognized my own pendent limbs or hammering heart. The dead reside as near as the past. Simon moved shyly inside me.

Namaste: The god in me honors the god in you. On our north shore silent retreat, the small group of retreatants greet one another not with words but with prayerful hands touched to the breast-bone and a slight nod. If my eyes meet another's, the electricity of speechlessness passes between us. It is unbearable; we look away, out over the surging expanse of Lake Superior. Or if we linger, sinking into the round, wet world of another's eyes, we splash at the bottom, lost to ourselves but more within ourselves than ever before. Here is the place where there is only one of us. Connection is potent, subterranean.

After a meal that is all flavor (curry, apple, rice) and no conversation, tea gets poured around. We turn our faces away from empty plates and burning candles toward the window, where birch trees and dangling bird feeders frame the lake. There is no opposite shore. Sky meets freshwater in an exquisite line. Steely carbon blue shifts to India ink, although the sun leaves fading blush marks in both air and water. Cupped between my hands—between each one of our hands—hot tea is steaming. I sip slowly. Together we drink down the sun, drink down the enormous lake laying its liquid self bare to the night, we take into our wells that stuff of which souls are formed and filled; we swallow, absorbing silver into our blood so that when the cups are empty and the windows dark but for two reflected candle flames and the blinking green light of a taconite mine down the shore, the whole silent moment is part of the bodies that stand, push in the chairs, and move to the sink to start the dishwater. Even there, swirling soap in the mugs, we are quiet.

I drink hundreds of cups of tea in a year, thousands even. From my morning reverie beneath the covers, dreaming along the train whistle's path, I rise, throw on a robe, and shuffle to the stove. I turn on the gas beneath the kettle. The tea I steep is ordinary. With milk it is murky, secretive in a mug, but still it is not that amniotic, great lake enigma, the collective unconscious in a cup, that I drank one autumn in silent company. It is merely leaves soaked in hot water, waking the synapses in my brain. I carry my cup to the porch. Hot ceramic warms my fingers and steam moistens my face.

At the edge of the neighborhood I hear a squeal of metal brakes and wheels grinding to a halt. Two boxcars crunch together, coupling at a joint low to the ground. I imagine the line of commuters restless behind the flashing red lights, and the grain car under the elevator's spout, filling with corn. There's no way to ride those shimmering rails of connection without cargo and an engine, without the blessed burden of the body. For now, this cup of tea I'll drink to the earth, to the farmers, the truckers, the conductors— to the bleary-eyed grocers and the scrawny girls at the register, to the tea bag, to the cup, to the potent liquid of this moment by myself, when I am so much with you.

House of Prayer

On any given day, this is how I pray: For the girl who loudly talks to herself on her way to the bus stop. For the clear half-moons of Rhia's nails I find between my sheets. For the woman riding an old-fashioned, flat handlebar bike with two potted vines flailing their tendrils in the rear basket. For autumn's first chill. For the boys beating each other on my lawn, who scatter when I scold them. For my answering machine's blink, for the press of a button, and my neighbor Annie's voice reading me her latest poem. For dust on the piano top. For the kindly, bearded postman who smokes a pipe, who slips a stack of envelopes through the mail slot and then bends down so Rhia can sniff through the screen. For squirrels scampering on the roof. For birdseed, scattered. For the teenager across the street taking some fierce anger out on his car, jumping on the hood, kicking the doors, pounding his fists. For these houseplants, for books filling shelves, for an empty table. For the woman who walks past each day at a quarter to four. For cookies and boiled tea. For honeysuckle twining up the house, flowering red. For Hero, the new Dalmatian next door, standing with front paws on the fence to look you in the eye. For silence. For the perpetual stream of kittens born in the neighbor's bush. For forbearance and hope. For the crowning moment when the mighty elm releases its halo of leaves on our street, suddenly saturating the air with gold. Rhia dashes madly across the porch trying to catch these drifting bits of holiness, while I do the same from my writing desk window. Afterward what has resided high in the branches all summer is exposed: a squirrel's nest of miscellany, open to the autumn blue.

ASHES, ASHES

I felt safe there because it was my home.

—*California woman who reentered her house
after it had collapsed in an earthquake*

Returning Home I

Strapped in the backseat of my parents' Dodge, I watched the moon migrate from above Grandma's driveway, where we blew kisses and my young father tapped the horn in farewell, across New Jersey, over the Tappan Zee spanning the murky Hudson, and into the streets of Tarrytown. The moon was a steady compass point, slipping behind shopping malls or sycamores then emerging again, pearly and round. God, I imagined, was like the moon—wide-eyed, protective, traveling over my right shoulder. The world was held safe in its light. The car turned east or west and the moon's cool white disc arched across the windshield, shifting the front seat shadows over the black vinyl of the back. Often I feigned sleep, listening to the pavement count its paces beneath our tires, watching through closed eyelids the orange streetlights sweep over our small, hurtling world. I kept secret the ritual of returning home, the final slowing on Route 9, my father's decisive left-hand turn followed by a sudden dip into our neighborhood, the car's heave over the gutter hump and down our driveway slope, the engine's sudden silence. Even awake, my limbs were too heavy for me to lift and so I kept my eyes shut, waiting for my father's arms to slip under my back, my knees; he hauled me up and into the house, screen door latching behind us. Home descended on me like the nightgown my mother slipped over my weary and waiting body. I was surrounded by dark walls and the circular song of swamp peepers and, after my mother's kiss, by sleep.

When did I become aware that the security of our green-shingled house facing the Hudson was an illusion? Twice our house was burglarized in our absence, the intruder crawling in an open second-floor window, stepping over an unfinished card game on the rug, making off with my mother's silver the first time, her jewelry the second. The sickening surprise of finding the front door ajar or seeing an unwelcome stranger's footprints on the carpet lurched in my stomach. I inherited my mother's worry as I never did her jewelry.

As my father climbed the pay scale, my parents' working-class foundations receded at an alarming rate; their concern for possessions was matched only by their guilt for having what others, including their own families, did not. In adolescence I acquired anxiety so potent that I confused it with prayer. Homecoming then was fraught with apprehension. Five miles away I'd wonder, Will the windows be shattered and salty air blowing in off the river? What if a train sparked the swamp into flames with no one home to call the fire department? It was easy to flip my worries into petitions. Please, God, let the basement not be ankle-deep in water. When we turned onto Pokahoe Drive to see the house still standing—when we unlocked the door to find the air inside stale—I felt relief, as well as shame for having suspected it otherwise.

Even this afternoon, driving from northern Minnesota toward the city of my adulthood, I felt carefree until the high-rises of Minneapolis punctured the foreground with their sharp, urban reality and I saw in my mind's eye, huddled beneath them, a diminutive, defenseless bungalow with mulberry leaves layered on the lawn and petunias dying in the window box. The more I love a place, the more that love is overshadowed by its potential loss. Surely in my absence the cat will have died. A storm will have blown down the evergreen and splintered the roof. Some prankster will have graffitied my garden shed. When a member of my congregation wound up in a psych ward, convinced the FBI was after her, I understood how swiftly the full scope of disastrous possibilities can encroach and sweep us into insanity. Pushing the speed limit, I took the freeway exit and drove down the grain corridor cutting diagonally through south Minneapolis. The same stoplights that give me no thought when running errands were endless and aggravating. None of us would be afraid had we not at some point experienced good cause for fear. I've seen fire rip through a building in a quarter hour, I know that the breath which gives us life is infinitely fragile, and I can't quite peel this knowledge away from daily living. On the other side of the railroad tracks, the houses of my neighborhood sat in quiet rows. And when I steered the car down the alley, between the packed garages and into my driveway, my homecoming was no different from a thousand others. Picked-over skulls of sunflowers nodded at the garden's edge. I fit my key into the lock, turned, and walked back into an uninterrupted life. Rhia flopped on the kitchen floor for a belly rub. The duration of affection she received was in direct proportion to my gratitude for her continued, purring existence.

Leave-taking is now an act of faith. I camp on weekends, retreat on the north shore of Lake Superior, return east every August to visit family, and each time I close the door behind me with trepidation. The faith I am learning is not in God's exclusive protection from suffering, nor is it blank trust that tragedy won't strike. Rather, it is like loving the inconsistent moon that streams through and through our traveling darkness. Within each of us there is a home, steadily holding the light. It's to this home I strive to return.

Bully

A YEAR AGO, following a tramp through autumn leaves, a friend dropped me off at the curb, then pulled her car away. The sidewalks were empty, the air gray. I climbed my front steps. From over my shoulder and across the street, words detonated: "Fuckin' lesbo bitch!"

Without looking I knew the source—a blank, second-story window in a house that's listing and losing chunks of stucco. The voice was young, male, grating. For a moment the words hung taut between our homes before dissolving into the neighborhood's Sunday quiet. I debated my options. Flash the finger? Cross the street, beat on the door, and confront this kid? I could have wittily instructed him on the distinctions between lesbianism and bisexuality, or between someone who's "fuckin'" and a single woman who's not. I should've called the police. This wasn't the first time he'd harassed me. I have a right to enter my house without malicious speculations about my sexuality broadcast in public.

Instead I bristled, pretending not to hear. This battle would be won by never engaging in the first place. Thus I stole the sting from his insults with silence. The screen door was sticky. I struggled with it, my proud back toward the vitriol across the street.

Had I turned, I would have seen a faceless window where a sixteen-year-old high school dropout spent his days watching TV and minding the neighbors' business. He was big, six feet perhaps, with a rolling belly and thick, pasty thighs. When I first moved in, he left the house three days a week with his backpack slung empty over his shoulder and walked up the alley toward the high school. More than once I watched him reach his backyard, hesitate, and return to the house, not to appear again until the next day. In the summer he used to play street football with other neighborhood kids. On a few occasions, he and his buddies sat on the curb a safe distance away and hurled epithets at me as I climbed into or out of my car with its rainbow sticker. The fact that he was now badgering me alone, from the safety of his bedroom window, made me wonder whether his friends had moved on.

I wanted to shrug off this kid's crude attempt to build his self-esteem; I wanted to enter my sweet home and lock the door against him. But once indoors, I knew his words had entered with me. Bitterness rattled my body. I turned toward the living room window to safely spy on his house. It is like a child's drawing, the two windows staring eyes and the door a surprised mouth. These days, the only time the kid ever steps outside, barefoot and in boxer shorts, is to retrieve the mail or have a smoke. He's the man of the house; his older sister and mother leave him on the couch and head off to work each morning, sometimes giving me a curt nod as I pick the newspaper off my stoop. I despise his life of frozen pizzas, pop, video games, daytime TV, and a string of smokes lasting from noon, when he rises, to midnight. He doesn't drive. I've never seen him with a girl. The descriptor quickest to my tongue is "loser." When he gets his hands on firecrackers, he prefers to light them in the house, open the front door, throw them randomly, then shut himself back inside before they explode. The blasts can continue off and on for hours.

Sometimes I pray that his mother doesn't keep a gun.

The flat-faced house swallows my neighbor, churns him in its dank digestive juices, and spits his anger into the street. When I lived in community, we used to complain that fellow community members always reveal to us those aspects of ourselves we like least. Peering toward this pitiful boy's screen-darkened window, I wondered whether I was frightened more by his hatred or my own. Shortly afterward I dreamed I was Dietrich Bonhoeffer; I'd been plotting to overthrow Hitler, and the SS was about to raid my office for incriminating evidence. I raced down the stairs toward the basement where I intended to burn my notes in the furnace. As I dashed across a landing, the neighbor kid was there, leaning on the railing, arms folded, feet bare, and flabby thighs stretched across the carpet. He observed my guilty pace and the papers I clutched to my chest. Panic rose in me—now there was a witness. His smirk showed that he would expose me. When I woke I saw that kid's counterpart in me, disdaining difference, submitting to inertia, working to feel better about himself by disparaging the neighbors. He's a wild card. He's the culture's baby, the one who would righteously turn me in. We watch each other's windows, looking for a fault or a failure and an easy way to feel secure.

Through the Dark Night

*A*s a girl I wrote the same way I lived—headlong, trusting heedlessly, impatient with handwriting in my passion for whatever came next. Stories unreeled themselves like dreams. Mystery infused the intersection of language and love. In sixth grade, Mrs. Russo passed out thin composition books with blue paper covers; she laid two sharpened pencils on each desk. It was a writing assessment: forty minutes to demonstrate our skills (to the Tarrytown school board? to the State of New York?) by answering the question "How do you spend your spare time?" or addressing a topic of our choice. It was a rare moment in my public education when I was provided paper and time to write whatever I wished. Mrs. Russo set a cooking timer ticking on her desk. Heads bent. Pencils began scratching, while overhead the fluorescent lights emitted their high-pitched buzz.

I dove. The narrative waters parted, and below the surface was a shifting, fluid world where skirts flowed around bare ankles, where pillars upheld a vast hall, where sound was magnified and emotions piercing and pure. The hall converged at a marble dais. I mounted the steps. The air was thick and dim; there was a swish of heavy fabric.

A stabbing "ping" from Mrs. Russo's timer jarred me. I came up for air, bewildered by the classroom's brightness. The clock's face was blatant and unbelievable. My grumbling stomach confirmed the hour, and so I set down the pencil. When Mrs. Russo collected the composition books into a stack, I was certain mine had an aura. All it would take to return to that mythical place was to fold back the blue cover and follow the loops and dives of my childish handwriting. Unlike the fantasies that spun themselves out for the duration of long car trips, here was a world to which I might return, which others could inhabit as well. Story held outside of myself the wonders I treasured secretly, within. My body felt light. Between wide-ruled pages I'd found, at last, a place where I might fully reside.

Today, winding up the stiff garden hose for the season, I saw my life (suddenly, fleetingly) not as a struggle to eke out a meaningful living but as the unrestrained adventure of a soul—a soft shadow fluttering in the mulberry branches. For an instant I was released from the human tether. Then the vision passed. My fingers were cold without gloves; the November air felt close. I wanted to catch that bird of a moment, its freedom and exuberance, and learn from it how to live. But it was too swift. I strained against consciousness for its memory.

Bits of stories appear to me like that, fragmentary and symbolic, clinging briefly to ordinary moments, whether or not I've put pen to page, and slyly shaping my experience. Dreams do the same thing, quirkily giving dimension to what I didn't know was shallow. And the Bible stories that have stalked me since childhood invariably creep into my vision's periphery. The stories we live with are as solid and unnoticeable as the frames a museum chooses to surround its paintings. Only occasionally do they come into focus, revealing the painting's shape, the surrounding room even, and the possibility that a new frame might better accent the shadows and light.

Three months after I moved to Minneapolis, I had an hour to kill before seeing my spiritual director (and, consequently, having to report on my current, shifty relationship with God); I was walking around a city lake when I felt a part inside of myself fall. On the outside, one foot preceded the other and geese scattered from my path. Inside, it was as though all my life I had been riding a mighty steed which, on a whim, decided to buck. I was thrown. Gravity yanked my heart down so roughly that it bruised and split. At least that's the image that came to me then, the story that layered itself on that moment, explaining my sharp intake of breath and clutched gut. Afterward, the depression that raged in me for a full year I blamed on the feisty and unfaithful horse.

Now I recognize the stallion as God, the theistic deity who existed outside of myself; it was a temperamental and unreliable mount from the start. The horse's image rode out of existing pain and the sensation of free fall brought that pain forward, into my awareness. I was lonely in my new house; I didn't know how to be angry; my choice to be self-employed gave me panic attacks. I suffered under the relentless stab of celibacy. The realization that God, the holy one I worshiped, didn't seem to care is what unseated me. I wanted to believe otherwise, but it was God who galloped away in that moment, flanks shining and nostrils flared with defiance.

The day is dark. Winter is setting in, and night tightens its vise on our overcast skies. The tunnel will narrow until solstice, and already, in early November, I'm claustrophobic. Will I survive squeezing through to the other end? The hose is in the shed, the water is off, leaves are raked over the garden, the clothesline is cleared of pins. I want to keep working but there's nothing left to do. The compost pile is frozen. The storm windows are up. Resigned, I enter my shadowed house where I will spend too much time in the coming months. It's not the cold that bothers me so much as the dark, how it eats up winter and forces me to go where I don't want—inside, into solitude and heavy quiet. I fight the shifting seasons. I am unwilling to accept how cycles of light and dark layer themselves onto my spirit.

And yet, regardless, they do. Our sixth grade class never got those compositions back. Some thoughtless assessor (a New York Regents officer? the superintendent? Mrs. Russo herself, with her lazy black eyes?) dumped the stack of composition books into a wastebasket and returned to us instead a roster of numbers. "Elizabeth," Mrs. Russo called me to her wide, meticulous desk. "You got a hundred. Excellent work."

I stared into her satisfied face for a moment before realizing that was all. There was no sign of blue covers on the empty wooden surface between us. My story had vanished just like my fantasies did, just like dreams dissipating into the dim corners of a bright day. The teacher's praise was meant to take its place. Suddenly the world was less trustworthy than I'd assumed. I returned to my desk feeling hollow, and strangely determined.

When I consider it now, a pattern emerges: the relentless pull onto the page balanced by its subsequent loss; the rapture of creation followed by destruction; the faith that comes with stability offset by wrenching doubt. It's easy to be starry-eyed about the spiritual journey until its underside makes an appearance, knocking you off your mount. From that eleven-year-old moment to this day, I've written fiercely, as though words might help me climb out of that place where our lives are splintered or manhandled or dismissed. It's what I'm doing now. I'm looking for the sacred, which supposedly brings us insight, connection, and love. But what happens when we are cut from the tree like so much dead wood and bundled off to the city compost?

Shortly after my metaphorical riding accident, I spent a rainy October afternoon teaching writing to senior citizens in north Minneapolis. By the time I pulled my car in front of my house, the cold was so penetrating I decided it was time to drag my winter coat down from the attic. Making my way toward the house, I avoided a puddle on the sidewalk. Then I noticed the string of bells that usually hangs from my screen door sprawled across the top step. I hung it back up. Had the wind been strong enough to lift the bells off their hook? Then I saw my office storm window leaning against the porch wall and shattered glass everywhere. The computer at my writing desk was gone.

Even before the shock of violation hit me (a hole punched into my house!), that familiar ache returned to the pit of my stomach—my writing, gone again. I had been working on a column for the church newsletter, and my memory of its meandering content immediately evaporated. The police arrived, swinging their hips up my front walk, brushing sticky fingerprinting powder over the storm window and making confident pronouncements: "Ninety-five percent chance it was a neighbor kid. Offer a reward. Put the word around the block." When they heard I was a writer, the round officer shook a fat finger at me. "Think carefully about who might want what was in that computer." I knit my brows, trying to figure out what movie he was mistaking for my life. In his eyes my words were powerful, worthy of theft, rather than the sorry mess of sentences I spin out like desperate prayer. I felt mildly flattered.

But no, my writing is always the casualty of wanton lawlessness. Some stranger craves my hardware, the megabytes of memory and the crawling insect screen saver that entertained my cat. The half-written column, backed up on the disk inside the computer, the rough drafts of my current manuscript, the lesson plans, inquiry letters, résumé—all airy and valueless compared with the keyboard-and-screen substance of a thousand dollar computer. But then I confront daily the worthlessness of words and excessive time that must be wasted to string them together. The theft of my writing, so many zeros and ones in an electronic brain, is just the iceberg's tip. Underneath, all the hope and longing and effort spent binding this life to the ephemeral Other dissipate into a sea of consumerism. Humanity is hostile. If something sacred resides in our feeble efforts to connect with creation, the world does little to confirm it.

Every loss brings up all other losses, including that first abandonment by the womb and the final forfeit of breath and heartbeat. My grief at losing my writing—*again*—wasn't so severe. But it triggered a serialized collapse of hope. Where was God? While I had no expectation that some sacred force might protect me from harm, I did have the belief, unquestioned since childhood, that God would never abandon me. Even as it grew harder to get out of bed in the morning, even as the pressure from tears grew constant, I held on to this belief. But my heart knew otherwise. The horse had thrown me, deliberately, then bolted.

The dark night arrived, low-hanging clouds pressing me against the muck. From the midst of it, despondency is as indescribable as ecstasy. It dwells deep in the body, moving idly like wisps of silt. Grit lodges in the smooth workings of your thoughts; it weighs down the baseline of your moods until even happiness drags and boredom loses its neutrality. The walls of your lungs thicken. Despair is not rational. Others suffer far worse, from far more unjust systems of oppression—war, poverty, abuse. Yet even in its mildest forms depression lodges within you as a cosmic experience of pain. It is an illness, beginning as the flu begins, with a dull, muscular ache and sweeping waves of nausea, reminding you of your inescapable mortality. Unwarranted, unwelcomed, speechless, still, it takes up residence.

Even today, on the other side of depression, I dream of strangers with evil intentions passing effortlessly through the locked front door of my house. Usually they are men carrying knives. I climb out of bed, naked. The robe I reach for is inadequate protection. Sometimes the intruders are teenagers looking for fun. Once I dreamed my goodly mailman barged in to give me a package, then sat on the couch to stoke his pipe. I stood in the kitchen doorway, flabbergasted. The gist of these dreams is the same. At any time, unannounced, some unwelcome visitor can invade my world. During my depression, the shadowy underside of God's comforting presence entered my awareness. Now I am skeptical I will ever shake it.

When I was in seventh grade, after I had decided to become a writer, Mr. Polliche assigned us autobiographies. "I want your life stories," he said. "Six pages." Tentatively, I began my first foray into memory, touching on the fire my family had witnessed in the San Gabriel mountains of California when I was five; the helium balloon, my name and address dangling from its string, I'd released in Tarrytown and later learned was found on Long Island; the birthday parties, best friends, and family vacations of my youth. As I wrote, the past grew animated and full. Memory fragments, placed side by side, fleshed out a portrait of myself that surprised me in its coherence. What began as an assignment grew into a mission. I was twelve; I saw my early memories endangered by the approaching onslaught of adolescence. If I could capture who I was at two, at five, at eight, *now*, through writing, that inspirited, youngest self might not get lost. My enthusiasm was dauntless. I wanted in my adult years to look back on myself with gratitude and awe; what foresight to have preserved these fragile memories! When I handed Mr. Polliche the rough draft and final copy in my best handwriting, the manuscript was forty pages long.

At that time, my feelings for Mr. Polliche were fueled by hormones and by a torrential love of literature which he, alone in my world, shared. I pined for him relentlessly, almost desperately. In Mr. Polliche I found a reader who pulled me out from under my shy veneer and boldly onto the page. I imagined his enormous hands cupped to catch all my fervent ramblings, and was sure that his capacity to hold my ideas was bottomless. Only now do I recognize how Mr. Polliche confirmed in a human way what I'd intuited earlier—that on the other side of the written page resides an audience of ultimate permission, encouraging our hand in the creator's work. I had written my life's story into this trusted ear.

Two weeks after the due date, Mr. Polliche turned to the class with a long face. "I've got bad news," he said. The gravity of his voice made my gut sink. I loved Mr. Polliche with such extreme, pent-up teenage passion that my thoughts went immediately to the worst possibility. He had cancer; he would die. I stopped breathing.

He continued. "I had your autobiographies with me when I stopped at the mall to run errands. Someone broke into the car. They took a bag of clothes that I was going to drop off at Goodwill, and a jar of change, and your stack of papers. I don't know why they took the papers. They probably just dumped them. I know it's not fair. I'm really sorry."

I exhaled with disbelief. Hours and hours of work, gone? I tried to recall the anecdotes I'd labored over, the events that had composed my life which I had then composed into a memoir, my first complete self-image. The memories were irretrievable. They had been stolen as completely as the pages themselves.

Adolescence crashed down on me in waves of fury and incredulity. How could writing, which felt so formative and *sacred* (the word I choose now for the sensation then) be so untrustworthy? In that moment, process peeled away from product. The point, I decided, wasn't to have the autobiography or even the memories. The point was who I became when I wrote. I would rebel against loss by writing even more; I would take this identity I'd discovered on the page and follow it forward.

Four years after my house was burglarized I still find shards of glass in the corners of my office. What fragments of my early childhood were relegated to a shopping mall dumpster, to billowing smoke, to the dusty realm of nonmemory? What kind of faith goes unchallenged? My computer crashes, taking with it the carefully crafted sentences that were *me* in the process of becoming someone new. Or my computer's life ends and the language with which the old machine recorded my thoughts is untranslatable by the latest contraption. Sometimes I see myself shedding scales of paper like the forty pounds of dead skin each of us loses in a lifetime—stories shluffed into the air where they are visible only when the sun angles in. God, Meister Eckhart wrote, is not found in the soul by adding anything but by a process of subtraction. All told, my lost writing is hardly my greatest grief. Nor is it close to humanity's profoundest suffering. I offer these paltry memories because the pattern of loss has offered itself to me, unseating my faith. Through them I seek the God of subtraction.

Years later, when I was in college, Mr. Polliche *did* get cancer—a brain tumor that killed him four months after the diagnosis. He was in his early forties, married, with a five-year-old daughter named Beth. I was in high school when she was born, and dropped by the junior high to congratulate him. "I named her after you," he told me, winking. *You are important to me*, he was saying. *I hope my daughter grows up to be like you*. During a lonely time, Mr. Polliche told me I mattered.

I was at a neighborhood garden party during a college break when I heard he had died. I was so grief-stricken I had to leave. It had happened suddenly, midsummer. Hardly anyone was notified, and so no students or faculty attended his funeral. A beloved teacher, a remarkable, calm man, was buried without public tribute.

Mr. Polliche had a long, bearded face, a lanky body, feet of astonishing length and hands so broad that he fumbled with stubs of chalk at the blackboard. Between classes, he stood just outside his door tossing his keys from one hand to the other, greeting each of us by name as we entered. The few times I was brave enough to look directly into Mr. Polliche's brown eyes, they seemed to encompass an intimate place in me, making me blush and turn away. After all, he was the first to read my poetry. The aching verses I wrote for the school contest brought his eyebrows up in a surprised arch. I won that contest—poet laureate of Washington Irving Junior High in 1983. My only copy of the poem was never returned. Long overdue, my unwarranted faith in adults finally began to crumble.

Even I have told sorrowful spiritual direction clients that an inability to feel God doesn't mean God is not present. The brimful heart, the leaping hope, the sly inspiration, and all moments when we experience and know we experience the pulse of creation are not the only times God is with us. The trouble is, I myself have depended on these moments as evidence that God exists. So my dark year was dark indeed. The sink of abandonment seemed just as trustworthy as earlier, happy moments, leading me to surmise that either God or my experience was capricious.

I took grief to my spiritual director. She believes, as purportedly do I, that others can hold hope for us when we cannot. My tears were profuse; I could see no end to the heaviness. "You've entered the dark woods," she said sympathetically. "But you must be halfway through."

I looked at her, skeptical. "What makes you say that?"

"If you were near either end," she said, "you'd see some light." I scoffed at her gimmicky metaphor. "Seriously," she said. "That's one of the perennial criticisms of Christianity. God doesn't bail Jesus out at the crucifixion. Jesus dies first, horribly, and then is resurrected. You have to go through the woods to reach the other side."

What the hell kind of God is that? At the opposite end of the forest perhaps I'd be stronger and wiser and bear all kinds of spiritual gifts. God, it is said, works when we're vulnerable and most open to transformation. But to someone in the muddy middle of things, that information doesn't help a whit. It makes suffering a blessing in sinister disguise, or a manipulative test of character, or a harsh remediation of our shortcomings. It means the sacred being turns its back during our most needy times, only to swoop down deus ex machina when the pain is over. I couldn't believe in a creator like that. The Christian story suddenly seemed misguided, even perverse. If God was a player in the passion drama, God missed his cue.

So my options were these: God didn't exist (but my experience told me otherwise!); God was hurtful or helpful according to some bizarre logic; or God resided beyond the measuring stick of my experience. "People suffer," my spiritual director said. "There's no getting around it." What if God was not so great as I'd presumed? "Perhaps God hurts when you hurt," she suggested. "Perhaps our suffering is God's great ache."

In the mid-1990s, I moved up to the north woods in order to write. It was a huge step, away from a tenured public school job into communal living and an artist's unreliable income. I pared down my possessions to a minimum, selling textbooks and giving away clothes in an effort to simplify my life. Friends caravaned everything I owned in a few cars and a pickup. We stored the furniture, bike, and boxes of books, journals, and photographs in a barn until my apartment was vacated.

The night before my final move, a car with a faulty ignition caught fire after the driver pulled in for the evening. Flames ripped through the wooden barn, leaping from one bay to the next until the area with my belongings was a fiery furnace. Every poem, every piece of fiction, each one of nineteen years of personal journals went up in flames. Even if I had possessed the short story I wrote for Mrs. Russo or my autobiography or prize-winning poem, they would have burned. Computer disks of drafts, of aborted ideas and polished, published pieces melted; reams of unorganized papers, notebooks, index cards, margin-scrawled books, all burned. I stood outside the circle of heat, too stunned to feel the extent of my loss.

The blaze heaved sideways in waves, then shot skyward. Its beauty was captivating, the tops of grand Norwegian pines silhouetted by rolling flames. The light was blinding, the roar volcanic. Even forty feet away the heat lapped at us. At the fire's white center was a glimpse of the sun's surface (a molten, slow-motion fever), and at the top, saffron fingers slashed the stars.

For three days the fire burned until only red coals remained, the rain spitting and sizzling on their open wounds. Finally it sank in: I had lost my writing. The firemen were able to drag out a few boxes of books with their covers melted together and pages soaked from the hoses, and one box of my journals, the script washed clean, the bindings charred. I climbed through the ruins moving beams and bicycle frames with a pitchfork until the soles of my sneakers were soft from the heat. Underneath was nothing but ash.

When you enter the woods of a fairy tale and it is night, the trees tower on either side of the path. They loom large because everything in the world of fairy tales is blown out of proportion. If the owl shouts, the otherwise deathly silence magnifies its call. The tasks you are given to do (by the witch, by the stepmother, by the wise old woman) are insurmountable—pull a single hair from the crescent moon bear's throat; separate a bowl's worth of poppy seeds from a pile of dirt. The forest seems endless. But when you do reach the daylight, triumphantly carrying the particular hair or having outwitted the wolf; when the owl is once again a shy bird and the trees only a lush canopy filtering the sun, the world is forever changed for your having seen it otherwise. From now on, when you come upon darkness, you'll know it has dimension. You'll know how closely poppy seeds and dirt resemble each other. The forest will be just another story that has absorbed you, taken you through its paces, and cast you out again to your home with its rattling windows and empty refrigerator—to your meager livelihood, which demands, inevitably, that you write about it.

The dark woods aren't malicious; they're just part of the landscape. For months the blackened foundation and burned trees stood witness in our woods, until the dump trucks came and hauled away the evidence. Then weeds sprang up, and a new barn, and saplings. Traversing that scorched piece of earth, I knew my loss had erased me. I staggered through without identity or belief. Mixed in with those ashes were the remains of God's omnipotence and my own continuity.

When people hear I lost my writing in the fire, they often ask if I've been able to recreate any of it. Incredulous, I try to imagine piecing together burned scraps, except that there were none. The words were no longer inside me, nor their form, nor their intent. I've heard of families (Salvador Dali's was one) who lose a child and then name the next child after the first. It's a pretense; that second child will never be the first, and will never eradicate the memory of the first child. The self of those prefire stories was gone, as was the God I'd known. For months I floundered, depleted by grief, forced by circumstance into a spiritual emptiness. Isn't that the state toward which we soul seekers strive? If I'd known, I would have run the other way.

"When you study Buddhism," Suzuki Roshi wrote, "you should have a general house-cleaning of your mind." For new truths to take root, we must first clear out the old. But sometimes housecleaning happens, whether we choose it or not. After the fire, my room was bare, and my back, and my beliefs. I could assume nothing. Because I'd just moved, the people in community were strangers and could not remind me about myself. It wasn't grief that crippled me so much as terror—at being nothing. I floated through days without the anchor of familiar objects or faces, without journals to mirror back my past, without God at the answering end of prayer. On what could I depend? My identity, bound up in the crude matter of the world, was itself questionable. I might not exist. God might be nothing. I heaved great gasps of air and flailed, grasping for something solid.

"We see the flying bird," the Roshi continues. "Sometimes we see the trace of it. Actually we cannot see the trace of a flying bird, but sometimes we feel as if we could. This is also good." After the fire and again during my depression, I *knew* I could not see the trace, the significance behind existence. I looked through air to the dark matter weighing the void and saw nothing. The bird was there, as was my body. Beyond that, all that gave life import had vanished. On the page, my handwriting unraveled its mess of ink, but the words held no meaning. I wrote without hope. I wrote the same way I breathed, using up paper and air because there was nothing else to do.

Everything can be undone. Today the evidence surrounds me, in hard, brittle stalks of black sunflowers, in stark branches, in dead grass and silent sidewalks and the fragile condition of my spirit. Not only that—everything *is* undone, year after year, the seasons relentlessly erasing and creating with general disregard for life and purpose. I want to close and lock the door against November, but the chill enters with me. Already the house is encased in shadow. Such are the inescapable conditions of this day.

Like pleasure, pain is universal. Suffering is part and parcel of creation, the very stuff of birth. In the heart of the barn fire I could see it: stunning destruction cracking open the jack-pine, a senseless, magnificent violence that has existed since the very beginning. This is our world. Suffering is distributed unjustly, and yet we all taste it. The birthing mother screams and the baby is stillborn. Or the mother births silently and throws the infant in the dumpster. Or the infant is healthy and loved and leads a full life, then passes away. When I was little, I had a dream where I chose to die by fire. A small closet off to the side of a room was filled with slips of white paper. I walked into the closet. The air was dry. Paper rustled around me. Someone calmly lit a match.

We can deny our pain, thereby inflicting it on others, or we can feel it—grieve, scream, thrash out in anger, berate God, and settle into the dull postpartum ache. Writers cavalierly say there's no such thing as a bad experience, only good material, and I picture the office paper mixed with human ash knee-deep on Wall Street after the Twin Towers collapsed: all that life, all that work. Is it really possible to transform such loss? Then there are the hours writers spend agonizing, crying, reworking pain into story. The pain doesn't dissipate; it just gets shared with more people. Nothing about life is fair. Nothing redeems suffering, not one esteemed man's crucifixion, not any story. Our bad experiences are good material simply because they are universal and true. The end product will burn, if not now then in the last days. What endures is a solid core, forged where our pain touches human pain, glowing red with transcendence.

I give the thermostat a nudge, then hunker down with a book—the sermons of Meister Eckhart, fourteenth-century mystic, lover of God's darkness. In the alley across the street, a crew with chain saws is working around one of the few remaining noble elms in the neighborhood. Between chapters, I watch the cherry picker probe the upper branches until sprawling arms are reduced to stubs and the trunk is sliced into chunks and lowered by pulley. "Whatever one says that God is, he is not," Eckhart wrote. "He is what one does not say of him, rather than what one says he is." Eventually all I see is sky. I want to start weeping from the very beginning because this too is God—emptiness, nothingness, eternal absence. What felt like abandonment at the beginning of my depression was really divine letting go. In a perverse way, granting humanity the raw experience of the world without sacred intervention is a generous act. At some point every parent grants children their choice and its awful consequence. The crucifixion story encompasses God's utter powerlessness in the face of human cruelty, and an enduring love that surpasses comprehension. "If I say, 'Let only darkness cover me, and the light about me be night,' even the darkness is not dark to thee, the night is bright as the day; for darkness is as light with thee."

I know nothing of God.

If writing can die so completely, martyred by circumstance, and its loss cause such grief, then surely stories have a life of their own and an indomitable spirit. Burned or stolen or published or tucked in a drawer, every piece I've written slips between the cracks of consciousness and sinks into my bloodstream. Half of who I am today is the stories I've written, only they reside in muscle and bone. They leap with electrical charges between neurons. Their oxygen feeds my breath. In the beginning they were words, but they have become flesh and dwell within me.

For most of my life I lived with a story about God as a being—a creator, a parent, a mighty horse I rode with reverence and unwavering faith. It was a good story; for a while it was true. But when despair knocked the wind out of me and the story galloped off, when absence seemed as much of God as presence, I eventually found a new story, perhaps more sound: holiness dispersed through substance and emptiness, no longer elevated, no longer elevating some nor debasing others, but rather under, in, yielding and common. As I see it now, it's a story within which the Christian story resides, and so both move and have their being in my body, whose feet will never again leave the ground.

Love is never wasted, and neither is a story. Whether or not its external life is cut short, a story works on the inside, shifting molecules, moving memories. The changes are so slight they appear only in dreams—I no longer swim to school holding my pencils and paper above the water. Or the changes float like a speck on the iris, my sight interrupted momentarily by a meandering fragment. "The universe is made of stories, not atoms," Muriel Rukeyser wrote, and the universe is expanding. Who is to say that all that interplanetary dust isn't really ashes of narrative? Or that dark matter isn't poetry, formed, finished, and forgotten, somehow laden on the void?

In the autumn of eighth grade, I played outfield for our gym class softball unit. I had borrowed a school glove—not the coveted kind, dark leather with stitched pouch between thumb and forefinger, but a Charlie Brown glove, cheap, bulbous fingers worn and cracked—and positioned myself a healthy distance from second base, safe from most of the action. But I had put myself in danger of those fly balls really good players hit, which fall from the sun-glared sky at impossible angles—falling the same way my teammates' hopes fell when they saw the ball heading toward me. Most of the time I stood with my hands idle, feet kicking tufts of grass as players ran the bases.

I remember this day in particular because it was hot and dusty, and because I walked into a ghost. It wasn't the ghost of someone whose life had ended; it was the ghost of memories layered one over the next, the way stone steps wear down with use or a table top, passed from generation to generation, bears the marks of meals. Only this was in the air. Lonely, unhappy, left hand sweating inside the glove and my back to the sweeping Hudson River Valley, I was suddenly aware of the history in that grassy, distant spot of the Washington Irving Junior High softball diamond—more than a century of clumsy eighth graders standing here, infusing center field with yearning—to catch the ball, to play the game, to fit in. Their restlessness charged the air. My presence, awkward in a T-shirt I'd outgrown, scratching mosquito bites on my arms, joined theirs. From then on, I was certain, the ghost of me in that moment would haunt outfield.

I wondered then, as I do now, if every instant leaves wispy trails not only in people's minds but in the very atmosphere, the landscape we walk on and the air we breathe. Some nearsighted kid stood up to home plate and struck out. If this was so—if I carry the story of my life around with me and leave a shimmering path behind like a snail—then perhaps one life, even an insignificant eighth grader's life, makes a difference. I sympathized with the kid on the other team, tossing the metal bat as though it mattered not an iota that he'd brought the end of the inning that much closer. The bat hit the sand with a clank, puffing dust windward. Most often we don't know it, I thought, but we're walking through other people's stories all the time. There's this pattern we lay over the world, and it changes things. "Back out!" shouted my teammates, and players expanded across the field, a lung taking in air. The sun was relentless. If we leave a story behind us whether we know it or not, I determined, then mine will be poignant. Happiness is fine, but it means more at the end of a hard story.

Wendy Tremolini, wry, wiry, star of the girls after-school team, stood up to the plate. I took ten steps backward. The pitcher threw underhanded, Wendy swung the bat, and with a metallic pop the ball was launched, its dirty white sphere growing smaller, until it was invisible against the radiant sky.

Only now I catch it, a thud in my palm.

The story of the soul's night is never wasted. Sadness is a wilderness we walk through, leaving behind a meager trail of bread crumbs. We can't retrace our steps to get out. We can only forge ahead, meet the witch, outwit her when we can, grab her jewels, and run. If we make it to the other end, the father who chose to abandon us is still our father. His compassion is incomprehensible. The evil stepmother is gone; we don't know why, but we suspect she would still be there if we hadn't come so far. The forest remains—dense, haunted, its shadow encroaching our vision's periphery. How familiar it now seems! The gloom still makes us shudder.

God, it turns out, isn't a character in the story after all. Nor is God the story's author, scribbling away our fates from that great desk in the sky. God is more the story itself, the universe spinning madly, fragments straining to connect one to the next, broken themes stumbling toward unity, whole chapters cut, each draft deepening the last, the entirety contained in every minuscule detail. Nothing is so horrific that it can't be held within a story. The metaphors are poor, the words inadequate. The pauses bear weight. Occasionally the story lends meaning or context to suffering. More often it tears open our hallowed humanity. That's when the bird rises, up toward the branches, inking the air with its luminous trace.

Lament

*H*AVING DREAMED LAST NIGHT of the Hudson River, this memory keeps washing up, so I write it. A few summers ago, I was in Tarrytown briefly when two Minnesota friends came to visit. I took Beth and Simin canoeing around Croton Point and walking through the Sleepy Hollow Cemetery. One evening, we went down to the Philipse Manor Beach Club for a swim. I wanted to share the Hudson as I loved it, to banish my friends' incorrect assumptions about pollution levels by immersing them in the river's current and seaweed scent. It was perhaps 8:30 by the time we ducked under the weedy rope that sectioned off the swimming area and pulled out past the breakwater. The sun was slinking behind a gleaming stratus cloud; the water's surface was seamless and oily in the light. We swam; we treaded water and talked; we lay on our backs and looked at the hazy August sky. Suddenly, it seemed, the sun had slipped from the clouds down behind the palisades. The water turned black. Looking toward shore where streetlights were coming on, I wondered what it was that kept us afloat over this deep enormity. Then I looked again. The train station was downstream, and the streetlights I now recognized were not those outside the beach club but a half mile north. The tide was coming in. Without any sensation of movement, the river had swept us north. Now it was thoroughly dark. We started swimming slowly, against the current, downstream, and it seemed to me that the world is always like that, filling you with amazement but then sweeping you into frightening territory, flowing upstream when you expect it to flow down, blanketing you with night, carrying you toward danger, all the while being this immense, silent body of water rolling on and on, buoying you until the end.

Winter Garden, Outdoors

$\mathcal{M}$Y WALK TO THE MISSISSIPPI takes me behind the brick elementary school through the community gardens, icy and dead. Even in early winter the plots reveal the gardeners' distinct personalities. There's a thicket of raspberry bushes, now purple-skinned and sharp; a row of sunken barrels filled with composted soil; a stark plot of sunflower stalks bent at the waist; a matted, yellow square of grass. Some plots have neat earthen humps, others are in rows, and one is boxed in, raised two feet—wheelchair accessible. When I walked here at the end of the growing season, I carried plastic bags in my pocket and harvested some seeds, garden thief that I am. I had memorized my favorite towering perennials and returned to them, then wooden and pod-heavy. I shook their skeletal tops into my palms until needle-sharp seeds or miniature globes rolled between my fingers. Now there's nothing left to pick. The rhubarb plants have gone underground. Strawberry leaves have hunkered, and an occasional pale, puckered stem of brussels sprouts or broccoli stands frozen, mid-rot. The earth is hard. When the wind blows across the city, stalks rustle and thrash, shaking seed rattles and sweeping brittle branches through dry air. I suppose the latent potential for growth in a dormant garden should bring me hope. Instead, all I see is the exquisite muscle of death.

Taking Time

SLOWLY I DISCOVER HOW MY HOUSE is situated in the universe. Within its walls I sail through the cycle of seasons, an explorer with my neck strained forward. The first time the moon woke me bolt upright by appearing under the eaves of my roof and spotlighting my pillow at four in the morning, it was a brilliant surprise. Now the moon sags in the southern sky, skimming over my neighbor's house where it can't possibly reach my bedroom window. The planet is turning. Moonlight blankets the rooftops and enters the backdoor like a thief.

I'm awake now. I'm paying attention. On this new day, the house and I have arrived safely at winter. Snow is piled in blue-shadowed mounds along the walk, the sky is blazingly clear, and I'm paused at my window. A bird feeder, which has hung from my porch eaves for months, today, for the first time, was discovered by a squirrel. He hangs from the wire loop by his rear paws, feasting upside down. Perhaps the two feet of snow on the ground has something to do with his sudden ingenuity. Certainly the snow and cold temperatures (six below today, the radio announcer tells me) have to do with the feast I'm indulged in, a day without commitments, hour after empty hour. Grand extravagance! I've found a windfall. I want to gorge until I stumble backward, stuffed with limitless time.

But I can't. Somehow the capacity to inhabit time loosely, easily, moving from whim to whim until the day achieves its organic form, eludes me. I'm unable to work—do my chores, lesson plans, phone calls—with an unburdened calm and responsiveness. Instead, I sit down to write and the weight of a hundred tasks heaves into my brain. I make lists. The more practical tasks bully their way into my creative space and taunt my every sentence. *That witticism performs wonders on your leaky basement. Wouldn't a letter to your congressperson prove more effective than this literary whine?* If I brush away the million to-do's and face emptiness, panic claws my chest. The day becomes voluminous and reeling. I fear that the creative drive, were I to submit fully, would consume me and render me an irresponsible citizen. Does my life have worth without productivity? I could write all day, or pray, but when my mortgage payment comes around those pages and prayers aren't legal tender. Time may be neutral, but some ways of spending it get valued over others until time itself feels moralistic and threatening. I don't know how to unwrap time as the gift it is, free and simple and inviting, without it inevitably corroding with exposure to the inimical world.

From my writing window, I watch the neighborhood children make their way to school. There must be a patch of ice on the sidewalk across the street; elementary kids bundled in neon pink and green reach the spot and then move nowhere, despite their exaggerated walking motions. They bump into one another and fall, disappearing behind the pile of snow that lines the gutter. Later, the high school kids emerge wearing letter jackets and no hats. They amble down the sidewalk at a pace I doubt my body is capable of any longer, after years of being pressed into productive service. The kids are so carelessly slow, I hope they will survive the half mile to school without freezing. I'm in awe. What is fearsome to me, to have all the time in the world, these kids take for granted. When I venture out for a walk this noon, I'll try going that slow. Is dawdling still within my repertoire?

I don't remember keeping that kind of pace as a kid, but I'm sure I did. Every pair of shoes I owned was worn through at the heels from deliberate scuffing. I do remember one afternoon in sixth grade, when I walked the five blocks from the bus stop. I was alone; my schoolbag was slung over my shoulder and I dragged my feet along the pavement. Ant hills erupted from cracks in the gutter.

Suddenly I stopped and stared at my feet. The distance from my head to my toes was astounding; I felt dizzy; I was sure I would fall. When did I get so tall? How would I ever survive the world from such an unrealistic height? Just as quickly the sensation was gone and my four-and-a-half foot body felt sensible again. But I was shaken. At any moment my memory of being two years old might take over, and my physical self would seem monstrous. Or, I speculated, my foreknowledge of being twenty would feel cramped in my eleven-year-old body. What was this within me that could mutate and shift? I moved forward again, heels scraping the cement. For the rest of the walk home I lived in the miraculous appropriateness of my body.

Each day is a body. I flesh out this one with the choices I make—to window-gaze, delight idly in language, then fling myself from the dishes to the laundry to the dust bunnies in repentance, chat with neighbors, run meetings at church, and heave myself into bed. One moment balloons with volume and the next is constrained, limited, cut short. What if I grow listless or bored? What if I die tomorrow? What if I live so long that my life ends in poverty? Except for these immediate moments in front of the bird feeder, time, like God, is shapeless and unpredictable. If I walk in the body of tomorrow or yesterday, I topple over. Instead I must learn again how to drag my heels—how not to panic when I come to a patch of ice on the sidewalk but rather thrust my weight forward, fling wide my arms, and glide.

It takes effort to dwell in time in ways other than the unthinkingly obvious. I first learned this when I was younger—ten, on a field trip with Mrs. Daly's fifth grade class. We were crammed in a bus that at first smelled of fresh rubber mats and plastic seats, but gradually acquired the pervasive odor of strawberry bubble gum. The noise reached a searing pitch before we pulled out of the school parking lot. Cynthia Robinson and I were lucky to sit together on the hump seat above the rear left wheel. Every time the bus hit a bump in the road, we went flying. The streets of Tarrytown were uneven and glorious.

Eventually we were careening smoothly down the highway. The bus noise had organized itself; the majority were singing "Ninety-nine Bottles of Beer on the Wall." It was going to be a long drive.

"Do you know what I do when we take car trips?" Cynthia asked me. She was the only kid in our class with brilliant red hair and freckles. She played violin in the Morse School orchestra and, unlike the rest of the orchestra, was good. For Halloween, she'd been Cleopatra with a wig of straight black yarn hair. I'd been Pocahontas.

"What?" I was interested. My family took plenty of long car trips. I had my own secret game, but I'd never told anyone.

Cynthia reached over me to point out the window. "See that metal thing?" she asked. We both watched the guard rail race parallel to the highway, while shrubs and ditches and hillsides smeared in the background. "I imagine this little guy with red shoes and a red cap racing on top of it. He just runs and runs."

I looked from Cynthia's eyes out to the thin silver edge. "Doesn't he get tired?" I asked. I imagined the poor fellow with such small legs trying to keep up with the bus.

"Nope."

"What happens, like right there?" I pointed to a break in the guard rail as we went onto a bridge. There was a dangerous six feet of weeds before a low cement wall began. Below us, the bus tires made a high-pitched whine on the grooved pavement.

"He just jumps. He can jump really far."

I saw him pumping his tiny arms, oblivious of the distance beneath the bridge, the tassel of his cap flying behind him. When the bridge wall ended and the guard rail began again, he leaped effortlessly.

Yes, this was a good game.

"Do you want to know what I do?" I asked Cynthia hesitantly. It felt risky to share our private, imaginary worlds. At age ten, peers were becoming moody and unreliable. I was beginning to be cautious with secrets, especially my own, because I'd seen them turned against me. But in this moment, Cynthia seemed trustworthy and eager.

She nodded.

"I make up stories. I say, 'What would it be like if. . .' and I fill in the blank."

"Like if people had wings?"

"Yeah, or if we could read each other's minds, or if there were whole other worlds living right on top of our world, only in different dimensions. And then I pretend I'm living there, and make up what would happen."

Cynthia considered this for a moment. "Hmm," she said, finally. Her eyes grew distant; I could tell she was playing a scene out in her mind, trying on my game just as I had tried on hers.

For a minute it was quiet between us, and then there was nothing—we were staring out the window, hypnotized by movement that always stayed the same. Our hearts grew still. The world narrowed itself down to that little runner who covered distance lightly or to the edge of unfolding in a what-if story, singular and present. In that silent place, time did not exist. Or if it did, it was a clean, concise moment big enough to sustain eternity. I know that we shared this experience because when the bus stopped, it jolted us both. The noise of our classmates hit us like a wall, as though we had crossed back through the sound barrier. "We're there already?" Cynthia exclaimed. It seemed like the bus had driven the entire length of a string, while Cynthia and I found a place where the string looped, its ends almost touching. We had leapt airily from one frayed end to the other.

And landed someplace new. A good meditation still does the same for me, hauling me out of the customary sensation of time into a nonquantifiable space pulsing with breath. The hours condense to a point. Often I rebel by avoiding meditation and its seeming lack of productivity. Or I strain against that black hole of quiet with my myriad monkey thoughts. Or, rarely, I let go. Is the world always so packed with eternity? Is it just our perceptions of it that are fleeting? Do I dwell in time or does time reside (caged, an eager animal) in me?

I hardly know what to think. Meanwhile, my culture cries, "Forward, march!" Time is linear, just like the accumulation of money market interest and the progression of public school curriculum and the growth of mold on my refrigerated leftovers. We fall out of the womb and race toward the grave. Time is clear—a clock, a calendar, a lifeline we draw in memoir class with significant moments ticked off in chronological order. We measure time in events and accomplishments. We don't have time to think otherwise.

Recently a friend challenged me to write a musical score of my spiritual journey, knowing full well I'd never composed music. "If you can't hear the melody, at least make it artistic, or rhythmic, or colorful." I drew my score with crayon on staff paper, my whole notes a deep purple, the rests in black and white, the chords leaping into the margins in rapid succession. Time became less a progression of events and more a composition. To get from this moment in history to that moment in the future, I might walk forward doggedly or I might slide down the decrescendo to the da capo, ending where I began. After all, it's winter over and over again. The seasons aren't moving anywhere fast.

We all have experienced time in its warped and limber form—in our dreams, those nighttime ventures off the charted map. I learned this when I was seven and my sister five and my mother first explained daylight saving time to us. It was fall, late on a Saturday night; we had just walked around the house turning the hands of our clocks back an hour, and then collapsed on my parents' bed. Apparently the entire country was doing the same thing. Marcy and I were confounded. Time was still happening, wasn't it? Who were we to tinker with the clocks?

My mother was exhausted. She lay on her back as though she had no intention of putting us to bed. "We don't actually get an extra hour," she explained with her eyes shut. Her speech was slurred with sleep. "We just measure time differently, so that the daylight is more in the middle of the day." Marcy and I looked at each other, perplexed. "This way," my mother said, the muscles of her face going slack, "little kids don't have to walk to school in the morning with blue paint."

For a moment Marcy and I puzzled over this latest mystery. Changing the clocks, the walk to the bus stop, and blue paint? I pictured a nation's worth of schoolchildren condemned to paint the morning skies because the evening before we had not messed with the mechanics of our clocks. Then we realized she'd fallen asleep and we burst with laughter. "What? What?!" my mother demanded, propping herself up on her elbows.

"You fell asleep!" we told her. "You said blue paint!" Those sloshing pails had appeared out of nowhere. In the middle of explaining daylight saving, my mother slipped into another time entirely, one that unravels in images rather than numbers, where fabulous leaps of logic and chronology still make a continuous story. There are no clocks to turn back in our dreams. There is no time whatsoever in dreams, but rather one event melted into the next, so that we wake with vague recollections of infinity.

No, time is not what we conceive it to be. Distance to the stars is measured in light-years. Humanity is a blip in the earth's history. What started as a day without obligations—an achingly blue sky—has stuffed itself with sentences. The squirrel leaps six feet from the feeder to the ground, landing heavily in the snow, and red-breasted house finches alight in his place. The school bus is gone. I could, if I wanted, walk around the block or knock icicles off the eaves or go back to bed. I could find a more profitable occupation, requiring my daily attendance and distracting me from fruitful leisure. Perhaps then I could get a new muffler for my car.

Instead, I carve out hours for prayer and writing. There's so much time! Only rarely am I able to enter it as children do, bloating the hours the way air expands a tire. In the summer when I was little, my friends and I wheeled our bikes to the top of Pokahoe hill and made odd rules for ourselves—only one push on the bike pedal, from the twelve o'clock position to six o'clock, and then no more pedaling! Whoever went furthest won. We sailed far too fast down Pokahoe's slope, turned a sharp corner onto Hemlock, passed the bus stop with its high tangle of bittersweet vines, passed Mrs. Kelly's house where I took ballet lessons, slowing around the bend until we finally bottomed out in the horseshoe curve of Birch Close, our bikes crawling by the inch until we lost our balance. Time for us was the distance we covered. And those moments we sagged into the kitchen, complaining to my mother that we were bored, that there was nothing to do, were the times our hearts had shut down. We were agoraphobic in this field extending forever, or to the beginning of school, neither of which we could imagine.

The results of adulthood agoraphobia are just the opposite: so much to do that time gets crammed. Out of fear of time's immense cavern, we judge it—quality time, productive time, wasted time—and turn our backs on its ambivalent vastness. Whatever happened to that elementary school construct "free time"? When I face the emptiness of another morning, why do I instinctively run as though from a fearsome God, giving my time away in the guise of earning a living and packing the remainder with errands and the hundred tasks of keeping house? I become socially acceptable, one of the many complaining that there's not enough time. It's easier that way, traveling along a timeline, crossing off events like a to-do list—in other words, taming the beast as is our culture's custom.

It's much harder to take the time I'm given and inhabit its nuances. The postman lumbers up the walk, frightening off the finches; he slides the mail through the slot and it clatters into the little box. The sun is midway up the southern sky. Looking down my walkway, the heaps of snow on the left are golden and those on the right are blue-gray. I've often thought a day observing the exchange of light and shadow on my home's walls would be well spent. Then I'd recognize which parts of this house face our mother star and which turn their back. The movement of the earth would reveal its quiet drama on the walls and floorboards. I'd witness a day, so simple, so long and full of splendor.

But I've never had the forbearance. Perhaps time is better known obliquely, anyhow. They say the soul is like that, a fickle thing, revealed not by a spotlight but in shadows. If I look at the length of this day through my peripheral vision, it's neither short nor long, empty nor full; it has no expectations nor prerequisites nor regrets. Through its impartial and generous nature, time emanates holiness. Thus our relationship with time is telling—it exposes our gods. Right now, the sunlight hits the piano at an angle, smearing the propped-open music, singling out the lowest octave and four keys below middle C. The performer is a brilliant ghost. The music of this moment is different from the next (the sun shifts up a half step), but each resounds with . . . silence, with continuity, with the passage of life. I can't bear to watch the whole concerto, darkness overtaking the keyboard while sunlight climbs the walls. I'll only catch glimpses. In a sideways glance, I see a shadow fly across the living room—a crow, possibly, winging its way to the backyard. I have no idea what time it is. But I suspect I've just seen the mechanics move inside the clock.

Only once do I ever remember looking time directly in the face.

When I was in college, a friend of mine had the key to the campus observatory. Throughout our senior year we took advantage of it—free access to one of the finest telescopes in Minnesota. Late at night, our walk from the library to the dorms took us past the squat brownstone with its silver dome curved against the heavens. If the stars were out, the dome glowed faintly. Marc and I would postpone our much-needed sleep and instead climb the steps, push back the huge wooden door, and enter a playground of stars.

On the evening of graduation, the planets were in conspicuous alignment, Venus, Mars, and Jupiter a perfect triangle within the scoop of a quarter moon. It was an auspicious sky, worth looking at more closely. After a dinner with two other friends and our families, Marc led us up the steps to the Goodhue Observatory. Moon and planets were bright enough to make the other stars blurry, but we didn't mind. We wanted to see the planets' countenance.

Immediately inside the front doors was the display room. It was round, with heavy oak cabinets encircling the base of the telescope upstairs. Glass doors to the cabinets looked in on dusty moon rocks and unremarkable meteor remnants. We mounted the creaky, narrow staircase at the back of the room, past professors' doors plastered with comic strips, postcard photos of Einstein, and murals of the constellations, to the top landing, whose light fixture contained a red bulb. The eerie glow was like the entrance to a temple. Marc inserted his key in the door, and we stepped into the breezy dome of the observatory with its elongated and wondrous eye.

When Marc opened the hatch, we were half indoors and half out, with only a cracked metal shell separating us from the expanse of night. I loved how that rounded cavern had a wind of its own. Marc pressed a button and great rollers at the dome's base began to turn, the aperture rotating toward the eastern sky. An eerie wail bounced off the rounded ceiling—the music of the spheres. We pointed the telescope upward and eastward, then took turns peering at Venus, ribbed and vibrant; the surface of the moon, pocked, textured with shadow. My grandmother stretched her sight upward, then my sister and parents, then each of my closest friends. When we spoke, it was in whispers whose sibilants skipped over the dome's metal surface. In the center of the room at the telescope's base was a wood-framed case with a single red bulb. There, weights sank and gears whirled, keeping time with the stars' movement so that the telescope wouldn't get left behind.

We swung the scope around to the Pleiades, then to the Horsehead Nebula in Orion's belt. The four of us friends had graduated; we would move into the world to teach, to get married, to go to graduate school; we would settle great distances from one another. Time would transport us into adulthood, with its preoccupations and accomplishments. But for now, we had converged in miraculous alignment. The light from those stars had traveled millions of years to arrive within our contraption of lenses. But it wasn't the past that we were seeing, pulsing and brilliant. It was the present, resonant with a shared history and the tug of what lay ahead. Time and space were conjoined in the eye of a telescope, through which the people we loved were gazing. Now was all that mattered—all, indeed, that would ever exist. Our home in the universe was these curved, metal walls, arched against the sky. The dome swung around with its high-pitched song. Inside the telescope's pedestal, the observatory's heart beat the pulse of eternity.

Returning Home II

FLYING, I CEASE TO EXIST. The shell of this airplane cabin, hanging perilously above the clouds, seems to be nowhere, and without location my identity is tenuous, temporarily suspended. I surrendered my unique personhood when I boarded this metal hulk, locked myself into the adjustable buckle on top of a floatation cushion, and was schlepped down the runway and thrust skyward. Surely air travel is an illusion. I imagine some god with air currents in its veins holding up the plane's big belly like a child's first swimming lesson. The pilots and airline attendants proceed blithely, assuming it's natural to defy gravity daily and to earn their living in this place between heaven and earth that is really no place at all. I am one among thousands crisscrossing the country, each of us lost in transition. We've willingly relinquished our groundedness.

When I was young I would stumble between the rows of seats to the airplane's miniature bathroom. The narrow door folded inward; I slid the latch to make the light come on. With my naked butt balanced on the metal rim, I waited for the familiar sensation of pee, its trembling release, until I was done without knowing it—the plane's vibration had obliterated the subtleties of my own body. What other parts of myself were missing midflight? Today I see the stretched, sci-fi images of spaceships traveling at light speed and imagine my body, slightly blurred and faded, spread at 10,000 feet across Lake Michigan. Will I ever put myself back together again? How many of my own light particles are falling like stardust into that blue expanse?

During our descent, whatever remains of me presses upward against my seat belt and departs through the top of my head. The body that bounces once the wheels touch the runway is deflated. The seat belt lights blink off, followed by a chorus of clicking release. I stand crook-necked under the overhead compartment until the aisle frees up, and then I move facelessly with the faceless cargo into the terminal, its trembling floor unsteady under my feet, and float down to the baggage claim where the crowd mills in expectation. One face comes into focus—it's Annie, dear poet-neighbor, recognizing me when I can't even recognize myself, encircling my body in a hug that convinces me I'm solid, her kiss on my cheek bringing me back into community. We bustle off to the parking lot. Annie tells me how wretched the weather has been. I describe the ice chunks I saw floating down the Hudson, and by telling her I retrieve the luggage of memory—New York's freshwater ice heaving on the tide and its city lights smeared across the humid sky. Annie drives upriver, past Minnehaha Park and into our plain neighborhood of stucco, snow banks, and neatly shoveled sidewalks. We park across from my house and lug bags up the steps. The bells on the screen door ring warmly; Rhia, fed by Annie in my absence, butts her head against the front door and then demands a belly rub. Relieved, I find that the house has been waiting, furnace idle, plants thirsty, the round dining room table eager to support two women's lingering conversation. What does it mean to be home? The kettle is on the stove. The desk is stacked with mail. The bed has dirty sheets but with my scent on them and the Minnesota wind. Home waits to hold you like a shoe worn to your flat foot; it brings you back into place, into your self, into your soul, which is altogether restored by the earth.

Winter Garden, Indoors

DOWN IN A CORNER OF THE BASEMENT, lined up in trays, seedlings are tunneling their determined route toward fluorescent light. Some balk at the basement's cold. Others are already hitting glass ceilings—shaggy tomato leaves flattened and wet, the poor cosmos I (mistakenly) started indoors back-bending their scrawny stems. Today I will transplant them into pots, bringing them out from their safe, warm trays into the bitter world. The raised grow lights will be a new goal to strive toward. I read that brushing your hand over the wee plants' stems once a day strengthens them to withstand the wind. Today I will begin petting my plants.

Of all the gardening seasons, this one, spent shivering in the dank basement, is my favorite. The February snows are heavy outside. Down here, coleus emerges with delicate purple splashes. I love the infant versions of plants, how most have an identity entirely separate from their adult selves, though they do give small hints of their future. Broccoli, with its oddly round first leaves, is already the dusty green that will later appear on the tiny nodules of vegetable. Cabbage sends flat leaves sideways as though making space for the monstrous head. The tomatoes, one inch tall, smell acidic. I'm struck dumb by their minuscule origins and willingness to grow in my basement. What astonishes me most, though, are my own hands, lined with dirt, agents of growth, without which this winter garden has no beginning.

Bad Bread

THE CRUST IS THUMBNAIL-THIN, a meek discoloration, practically square but for its curved top edge. Apologetic for its very existence, the crust yields to every pinch and poke. Yet it is resilient because inside the slices are bright white and boastful, so uniform, so American! Each can be depended on to be just like the next. No other bread rivals its convenience (my corner store stocks shelves of it, plastic wrapped, stacked like foam bricks) nor its price. Up on Lake Street there's a bakery outlet that sells day-old loaves for forty-nine cents; "Get your buns in here!" the sign demands.

Bad bread bends under the pressure of the buttering knife. In a sandwich, tomatoes turn the slices soggy and loose, jelly stains the sponge. This bread has no smell. In chic, high-priced bakery chains, bad bread will borrow a scent—rosemary sprinkled on the crust or roasted garlic baked into its folds—but the bread itself lacks the pungency of a body emitting its own odor. Bad bread is an addendum to soup or a means for conveying peanut butter to the mouth. It is never a self-respecting food, confident of its place at the table.

For years I hesitated to call Minnesota home because of the scarcity of good bread. How could I settle here if I'd never be deeply nourished? In New York there are still old-world, family-owned bakeries, and delis that boil their bagels. Really I was looking for a duplicate of Alter's, the Jewish bakery in the Hispanic part of Tarrytown. Every Sunday after church my family stopped there to buy loaf of rye. It was a supply bakery, and so the glass cases were mostly empty. The walls were white without decoration, giving the shop an abandoned feel—a few almond cookies on a plate, a dozen bare loaves on the shelf, and one kid in an apron, his dark hair standing on end. The slicing machine had a crank and two dozen toothy saws. In the winter, heat from the brick ovens below street level melted the snow on the side-walk into slushy puddles.

The ovens made the crust thick and tough as rawhide. On the drive home my sister and I ate the heels that would otherwise get lost and blackened in the toaster; we ripped them with our teeth like wildcats. Thus we attacked the loaf from either end, next eating the small, round slices that weren't much good for sandwiches. Their insides were fibrous, brown, speckled with caraway seeds. Pockets of air created craters large enough to stick a finger through. On an occasional Sunday we bought the loaf right from the oven, which meant it couldn't be sliced; it sat on my lap, warmth seeping through the brown paper bag, through my dress and down to my skinny knees.

At home we toasted the rye for lunch. My dad smeared his with seedy jams, while I always had mine with butter drooling through the air pockets. Toasted, the bread had a darker beauty, the baked dough bronzed and crispy. Two slices were a substantial meal. Afterward, I sucked the butter from my fingers.

When I try to remedy my bread cravings by baking my own, the results are mediocre. Sure, the process is gratifying—rhythmic kneading, the rising fragrance of yeast, how my house grows grainy, warm, and old-fashioned as it bakes. But my quest for thick crust often means bread the weight of boulders; my attempts at textured flesh result in doughy, unbaked lumps. I've made minor strides with French loaves, whose crusts respond well to baking over pans of water. And my oatmeal bread has decent flavor if I ignore its soft crust. But as a rule the bread I bake is bad. I eat it, begrudging the hours that went into its making, my stomach full but unsatisfied.

My Twin Cities friends respond to my vestige of East Coast snobbery with the patient conviction that I am wrong. They send me across town for halvah from St. Louis Park or for Oslo bread at Ingebretsen's; they bring me baguettes it takes real muscles to tear in half, and they flash vindicated smiles. When I found an authentic French bakery hidden among the warehouses north of my neighborhood, I finally conceded. The boulle, semolina, and caraway rye are solid, respectable creations. When you tap the crust, it's like knocking on a door where someone is home. You know you'll be fed generously. You work up a sweat sawing your way in. Your slices get caught in the toaster. Like all that nourishes us deeply, this bread is *bad*; it draws attention to itself, takes up space, requires time, demands your money in some shady part of town, and, when you finally take it into your being, fights back with crusty passion.

Scratching the Surface

STILL BLOATED WITH SLEEP, I stumble into the bathroom where the paint jolts me awake. The tub is a black-and-white checkerboard with the claw-foot toenails garish red; yellow lines punctuate the wall below the waist-high molding and red zigzags march above; fat, white spirals swirl across the green linoleum floor. It's insane. During the day I enjoy all this primary energy, but the colors are too much on first waking. I inherited the décor from Frank, whose interior designs have a whimsical flair. When Frank lived here, he painted the walls colors I'd never choose but have come to love—a pale, still-lake green in the living room, vibrant blue in the study, lavender for the bedroom. In the bathroom I'm less certain. Today I refuse to flip the light switch. I sit hunched on the pot, eyes closed.

In the bathroom I want to slump away from my surroundings and into my body. Isn't that what the cool rim of the toilet invites, and the bowl underneath? In the throes of my current spiritual malaise (I'm feeling shallow these days and don't know how to connect with the pervasive God I now believe in), I want to take my comfort here, where nothing is asked of me beyond bodily functions and ablutions. Porcelain, tiles, mirror, paint, the bathroom's hard surfaces bring me to my surface. In the dark, I step over the tub's high rim and enclose myself in shower curtains. The hot water washes away awareness of what's outside my skin until I'm just a collection of limbs, lungs, and leg hairs. Steam fogs my vision. Here in the bathroom, I can slip into the dumb physicality at the base of my being.

The sleepy peace I achieve while lathering up is remarkably easier than the moment a half hour later, when I will strike a match, light the candle, and try to meditate. Unlike showering, the practice of meditation is deceptive. You expect depth and meaning; you expect enlightenment, when in fact you're on your knees before the candle with the roar of the forced air furnace blowing through your brain, the cat whining to be let out on the porch, and a thousand responsibilities piling stress on your day. You realize how trivial most of your thoughts are. The Buddhists say, let your thoughts pass through like clouds, and you do, but it's a stormy morning. If, with practice or a stroke of luck, you enter that eternal cavern of quiet—if the furnace stops with an exhaustive sigh and the house suddenly prickles with emptiness—you find yourself not at the bottom of some sublime pool but rather on its surface, dark, taut, vibrating with every sound, attuned to the temperature, the slowing movement of air, the pressure of your blood; in other words, intensely aware of the world's physicality, sheer and unremitting. You no longer reside in your mind, framed by language, but rather in your skin with its animal responsiveness. If there's wisdom in such an experience, it's not the kind you can boast about.

My mornings of successful meditation are few compared with my showers, always hot, always clear of extraneous thought. The sheen of wet cleanses me of identity. I enter that watery, prenatal state, where my vague memories of sacred origins were formed and for which I'm always yearning. Eventually I must turn off the water and emerge from the shower-curtained womb. The air is laden with moisture; I keep the door closed to create a temporary sauna so my transition isn't as harsh as it might be otherwise. Finally I'm awake enough to turn on the light, pat my skin dry with a towel, and take in the crazy colors.

All this comforting steam leads to a disappointing result: the paint is peeling from the walls. A white leaf curls up by the ceiling, exposing pale yellow lath and plaster; cracks cascade frantically toward the toilet, and a chunk of Frank's black-and-white checkerboard has broken off the tub. The brief oblivion of my shower, instead of leading me to enlightenment, is producing an overwhelming homeowner's project. All the signs point away from profundity toward the surface, with its chipping paint and mundane demands.

This situation reminds me of the deteriorating walls at my church, where chunks of plaster have been rumored to fall on choir members' heads and the paint, where it's not peeling, is faded and stained. The church trustees recently launched a fund-raising campaign to give our hundred-year-old walls a desperately needed fresh coat. It's been an uphill battle—painting the inside of even a small church, with its peaked ceiling and choir loft nooks, is a $14,000 affair, and our congregation is reluctant to invest so much in appearance. Members would rather donate money to outreach than to furnace repairs or a new roof. We work under the assumption that, given our consumer culture's obsession with appearance, possessions, and inattentive living, the call of Christ is toward what matters most: working for peace, advocating for the poor, building communities, healing relationships. In other words, faith steers us away from the superficial toward the stuff of substance.

At the end of a service a few weeks ago, the trustees paraded around the sanctuary's periphery with doomsday signs proclaiming, "Repaint! The time is near!" I laughed aloud. That morning it was the trustees' message and not the pastor's sermon on forgiveness that struck my struggling heart. The trustees are practical people; they scurry around changing lightbulbs, setting mousetraps, and fixing vacuum cleaners. They know we're more generous if we're chuckling when we reach into our wallets. A fresh coat of paint not only looks good, they instructed us; it also protects the plaster beneath from the ill effects of moisture and helps the building maintain its integrity. Sitting in the pew, I moved my bathroom project up a notch on my to-do list. I'll concede and install an exhaust fan. I'll have to sand down the flaking paint, do away with Frank's blatant stripes, and figure out my own, subtler form of bathroom art—ocean-toned sponge painting, perhaps, or conservative cream with batik fabric curtains.

The trustees' practical demands are refreshing after a service on repenting sins and forgiving others. I won't deny the merit in embracing human weakness; it is challenging work that expands our capacity for love. But the discipline of repentance doesn't help much when we're haunted not by our own shortcomings so much as God's seeming inability to show up. I find more hope in the commonsense theology of the trustees' announcement. Their call to "repaintance" asks us do-gooder Christians to get over our selfless, otherworldly goals and actually see what's in front of our noses. Attention to the surface—recognizing what we have, calling it good, and working to preserve it—has inherent value. "Turn from your moralistic striving!" the trustees might preach, banging the pulpit with a toilet plunger. "Pay attention to what's at hand."

What's at hand for me is emptiness. For months now my prayers have been hollow, my well of insight bone-dry. And there's no sign that this isn't a permanent condition. What used to feel richly textured (a walk around the block blessed by sunlight, a moment of silence, an unexpected phone call) now skips the surface. Does anything have meaning? The wintry earth is comforting because its stillness, while perceived as eternal here in the Midwest, is in fact seasonal. The only reasonable explanation for my frozen heart is its own orbiting retreat from the sun.

So I lean against the rim of the bathtub, attending to what's at hand. The skin of my cheekbones is coarse, my forearms itch, and my knees are flaky and white. This is the hazard of dry Minnesota winters and too much pounding water. I slather myself with lotion—the worried muscles of my brow, my nose's bony bridge, the jaw bone, the shoulder blades, the forearms and overused elbows. God's immanence once seeped like oil through the pores of the world. Now I'm all dried up and must myself apply the salve.

There's a story about a woman who felt intense devotion for her teacher and chose to honor him by pouring extravagant perfume over his head. The other followers were displeased because the perfume could have been sold for a great deal of money to feed the poor. They scorned the woman and called her wasteful. But the teacher responded, "She has done a beautiful thing to me. For you always have the poor with you, but you will not always have me."

I can't bring myself to write off the lesson in this story by saying that the teacher was Jesus and of course someone as elevated as God's Son deserves expensive perfume. Instead I face the challenging notion that the teacher represents that which is wise and sacred—God incarnate—within each of us. When the woman cares for this presence, honoring it with lavish attention to its physicality, some imbalance is set aright. We are to tend both the temporal and the eternal. The story's surprise resides in the flip-flop of our expectations; it's human suffering that's interminable, while the manifestation of God comes and goes. Per-

꩜

haps my current blindness to heart and meaning calls me to attend to what's temporary—this skin I live in, untouched by rich perfume because, thus far, I have denied its worth.

I lean into the bathroom mirror, framed in a wooden medicine cabinet with a latch that makes a lovely snap as it closes. There are flaws in the glass; no matter how hard I scrub, the mirror never appears clean. The time I spend in front of the mirror is all facial—brushing teeth, slipping contact lenses onto my eyeballs, tweezing hairs. On most days my response to that reflected face is functional. I see stray curls to be tamed with a comb. Teary, I dip my pinkie finger under my eyelid to retrieve the errant lash. When I was little I sometimes bent close to the mirror to see its quarter-inch depth, the shiny paint on the underside of the glass. There's not much there.

Only rarely does it occur to me to see the image in the mirror as *self*, as the being that represents me in the world. She's flat; her left and right sides are reversed; she's not as beautiful as I'd like to imagine. Even after a comb is run through her hair, strands stand awkwardly on end. Her skin, while naturally blushed, is never quite free of blemishes. I'm intrigued by her eyes, which are supposed to be windows into the soul. Except I can't read them. The black pupil is an expressionless student, the gray-blue iris reflects light abstractly, avoiding my attention, and the whites, with their thin threads of blood vessels, reveal only weariness. I can't get inside.

The only time I glimpsed beneath my skin I was shocked by how much substance was there, and how little spirit.

I'd been suffering from endometriosis, errant endometrial tissue growing outside my uterus. The surgeons did a laparoscopy by making three small incisions in my abdomen and probing inside with minute lasers. Before they began vacuuming endometrial tissue off my bladder, they took a photograph, as I imagine it, with a camera smaller than the ink cartridge of a ballpoint pen. When

I woke from the anesthesia, they handed me the print as though it were my trophy for surviving the ordeal.

I tried to get my bearings inside the image. Pregnant women pore over their sonograms in the same manner, searching for the limbs and tucked heads the doctors tell them are there, trying to transpose this strange, shadowy figure onto the kicking weight of their uterus. The colors of my gut were rich, grotesque, otherworldly—the smooth coral balloon of the bladder, magenta walls textured with blood, and, malignant, growing where it didn't belong, a violaceous splotch with rust and maroon speckles. I was stunned by the alien nature of my innards. With effort I could conceptualize this packed, vibrant realm existing inside me, underneath the tight, shaved skin of my belly. But I couldn't sustain the image of myself as a sausage stuffed with organs for long. It was too inexplicable, too solid. In order to crawl out of the hospital bed and get on with life, I had to return to my old illusion, that who I am resides beyond the surface, that *self* is a dependable, indivisible unit made mostly of wispy thought.

Today, when my malaise is less bodily (some rift in the spiritual connective tissue, I suspect, or a heart valve blockage of the metaphoric variety), oddly enough it's the world's enduring physicality that brings me comfort. The bathroom reminds me that, if nothing else, at least I am this body exerting its supple presence on the world. The porcelain sink presses cold into my hips; I blink at the mirror and run a comb through my wet hair. Reflected in the glass are the wall's red zigzags and a face simultaneously familiar and inaccessible—as much a mystery as any profound dream or mystical communion. Soon I'll have to revise how I see the surface so I can know it, not as a skin for essence—a container for life's breath—but as holiness itself, as part of the unbent continuity between spirit and matter. By tending the temporary, we touch what's eternal.

For now, water courses through copper pipes beneath the floorboards; it runs over my toothbrush bristles and exits through the city's trusty sewage system. Down in the basement the furnace kicks in, blowing warmth up the ducts to the bathroom vent, where it stirs the moist air at my back. Hidden movements of water, waste, gas, electricity, air, and the slow peeling of paint all conspire to make this moment, as spit swirls down the drain, as I hang my towel above the vent, as I turn the doorknob and, naked, enter a blatant, bitter day.

Returning Home III

FROM FRONTENAC, a river town in southeastern Minnesota where I've taught a class, I drive north in the early evening, the road curving between bluffs and tucked-in fields seeded with corn. I follow the route the Mississippi has carved into the landscape, only upriver, going home. It is early spring; the trees look surprised to be leafing and the sky is fearsome, black storm clouds racing across a plaintive blue. When the sun slices through, the valley is blinded with gold. When it is hidden, the world is threatening and rain spits at the windshield. I alternate between wearing sunglasses and turning on my headlights. Occasionally, white cumulous clouds pass jauntily in front of the thunderheads. Hawks ride the rising air currents between bluffs.

In Red Wing I glance between brick buildings down to the river, slick and tidy between narrow banks. The Mississippi is determined and secretive. Leaving the final bluff behind me, with its looming limestone cliffs, I rise from the wooded valley, the car straining against the incline, until plains of black soil crossed by the delicate green lines of new soybeans stretch on either side. Here the weather pans out in full drama: fierce black against blue, shadowed sheets of rain in diagonal swaths across the horizon, blinding sunlight on willows and silver maples by a creek bed. My heart is not big enough to encompass this sky's paradoxes; it strains with too much beauty and terror. The storm clouds move in and I'm driving through a downpour, the wipers frantic against my windshield, lines in the road barely visible.

When I pass over the bridge at Hastings, the Mississippi is steely, churning, rebellious. The road climbs again, then widens; I pass sleazy dance clubs, gas stations, and, as I near the city, an onslaught of sprawling megastores and parking lots. West of the highway, a rail line glints among ragweed and dandelions. I catch a brief glimpse of the river where it flattens between swamps and rotted trunks; it is so wide it seems to have lost its embankment. Then I rise onto twists of highway, turning west toward St. Paul with its electrified billboards and cathedral dome surrounded with scaffolding; I dip into the bowels of the city and emerge from between cement sound barriers at my exit, where I stop for a red light. Above me the sky is lumbering except for the southwestern edge, which is as brilliant as the afterlife's gateway. The Minneapolis high-rises are magical. On the road bits of fluff— cottonwood fibers and the silver puffs of dandelions—move inches above the concrete in an invisible stream. The light turns green and I drive south then west, across the Mississippi once more where it lies privately between the cities, calm and confined. I'm almost home; I turn into the neighborhood just as the sun emerges within the canopy of ash and sugar maple arching over the avenue. The world is freshly washed. Even the back alley weeds between cement and stucco walls are luminous, even the crabgrass in the gravel driveway. I'm home, just as the sun ducks behind my neighbor's garage and my garden (narcissus, purple and white crocus, tulips) is washed with shadow. The grass is wet. I slip my key into the lock and turn. I'm home, where the roof shields me from rain and where walls contain me against all this dissolving splendor.

BUILDING MATERIALS

God is at home;
it is we who have gone out for a walk.

—*Meister Eckhart*

Penny Friend

*A*NNIE, MY NEIGHBOR ONE BLOCK OVER, bends down to the curved rut running the length of the alley and scrapes a penny out of the sand. She brushes its scratched surface against her blue jeans, then presses it into my palm. "You're the lucky one today," she says.

I slip the rough penny into my pants pocket, laughing at our odd ritual. It's not strange that Annie bothers to pick up a penny; she is Buddhist and a poet, a woman who treasures details and is as frugal with resources as she is with words. Even one tarnished cent gains significance by our attention. What is strange is that, week after week on our eight-minute walk to the café, the pennies appear with regularity, sometimes even nickels or quarters, and over the years we've placed in each other's hands enough to buy a muffin or cookie. Our friendship follows this trail of meager fortune.

At the café, we take out our notebooks and write. Thoughts still cost a penny apiece; with inflation, they're worth less today than ever before. And it shows. Our society invests in action, and the choices Annie and I make (to observe, to write, to practice our respective contemplative paths) receive little compensation. Still, the world is planted in pennies, as Annie Dillard writes. Treasure is out there for the taking. I collect mine as copper weight in my pocket—the slow unscrolling of words, an afternoon of liberty with a friend.

Thoughts on the Threshold

LAST NIGHT A SPRING GALE whipped across South Dakota and the flatlands of Minnesota. Minneapolis was buffeted, blustered; every tree bent eastward and last autumn's leaves plastered themselves against the sides of houses. I walked the two blocks home from the movie theater behind a newspaper page flying along the sidewalk at ankle level. Aluminum cans rattled in the gutter. The roar of spring rolled over the sounds of traffic and trains and filled my brain. I felt my body—the whole city, even—pushed forward toward an unseen edge.

Across the street from my house I paused. The small white stucco bungalow could have been any old house on the block—squat and neat, a light on in the kitchen, a few too many silvery exploded dandelions shaking their heads on the lawn. The front yard pine was disproportionately (in this weather, dangerously) tall. Above its bent tip the sky was from a picture book; splotches of orange clouds moved eastward, exposing then obscuring the naked dark.

I entered my hunkered-down house, took off my clothes, and went to bed. The attic door struggled to be free of its frame; following the winter months, I'd opened the upstairs window and now the air in the crawl space above me was alive. In the backyard the wind chime rang at a panicked pitch. A breeze seeped through the window beside my bed and I pulled the covers up to my chin. Just as my spine relaxed into the mattress, the screen door to the porch flapped open and slammed; my cat sprang to attention, her wide eyes meeting mine across the bed. The wind was rattling our cage.

A few winters ago, when all my windows were closed, I had a dream that my body was a wind tunnel, an empty vessel with no bottom or lid, and the air rushed in from my feet, through my torso, and out my head with a low roar. The sensation was so stunning it woke me. I lay still, my heart hammering as I tried to clear sleep from my brain. What had happened? I reached over to Rhia and let her bathe my wrist, her coarse tongue connecting me back to consciousness. But then my heart leapt and it began again, wind rushing pleasure through every bone, shaking me from the inside out, from the bottom up, a sweep of ecstatic energy passing from some mysterious place to another with my body as its conduit. My cells were transparent to this invisible, resonant wind. My ears roared. I wondered if Rhia felt the vibration through my hand against her fur. My neck was resting at an awkward angle but I didn't dare move for fear the wind would stop. I remember thinking, *Shouldn't my spine be aligned for this to happen?* and then being surprised that my thoughts were so mundane while energy streaked beneath and through my skin. Finally I adjusted the angle of my head. The airstream continued—a few seconds? another half minute?—and then subsided, leaving me breathless. My heart beat violently. The dark house was silent. For the rest of the night I lay alert and sleepless.

How near, exactly, is God? It was easier to ask this question before a dream-time bodily gale made my skin prickle, when wind was only a meteorological force thrust against my house. Then I could say that nature rides her laws steadily. However it happened, the world was set in motion and spins in obedience to those primal, unfailing principles. But now that I've felt that wind tunnel, even the real storm buffeting these walls seems to leap not from high pressure fronts causing atmospheric turmoil, but rather from some other inspirited place—wind on a mission, wind out to make itself heard. We think we know this weather, but we don't. At some point the obedient air blasts into your very bones, and then you no longer recognize what it is you've been breathing since your borning cry.

In the morning I wake to the house groaning like a ship at sea. When I first open the blinds above my bed, the dimness of the room doesn't change. The sky is temperamental, steel gray and threatening, and then suddenly in a burst of goodwill a patch breaks into blue, making me think, *Surely this day has promise.* But soon the room is swathed in shadow again and I slink back into the flannel sheets, resigned to the glum light. For a half hour I listen to pine branches thrashing out front and the overgrown mulberry scratching at my kitchen window. It sounds like the wind is searching beneath the house, trying to lift it from its foundation. Perhaps my sleep weighs the house down. No need to risk rising.

Rhia is braver. She arches her back in a feline yoga posture, then pads over to my chest. The orphan of two alley cats, Rhia is large-boned and brawny; her rump settles between my legs and her tail brushes the tops of my knees. She rests her chin between my breasts and purrs. I've heard of a form of yoga that awakens the energy in the fourth chakra, that space at the center of the chest, until your heart is purring. It hardly seems possible, except these days I'm less sure I know the body's full repertoire of sensations. With Rhia's motor going so close to my skin, I can imagine what it must be like—a fluttering from the torso's depths spreading warmth outward, upward, until every inch of the body thrums.

I fantasize about kundalini in the same way. A Sanskrit word for "coiled up," kundalini is the life force said to sit dormant at the base of the spine until spiritual practice releases it like a spring. I suppose it spirals upward, wrapping one's innards in a tornado of sensation until it crests at the skull's crown. The yogis say such a thing is possible. Was this the source of my internal straight-line wind? Apparently sacred energy can sweep us off our feet. If kundalini is the equivalent of spiritual orgasm, my Protestant tradition is frigid and impotent. We have no mythology to spark the physical imagination nor the language to give it words. Irrevocable, indisputable experience continues to unleash mysteries beyond those I've been taught. I grasp at any explanations I can find.

"This world is not conclusion," Emily Dickinson wrote. The thick walls of my flesh beneath the feather comforter, my hand as it reaches toward the cat on my chest, rising and falling, and the plaster walls of my home moaning in the storm are not the closed covers of a book. How I've experienced reality thus far is but a fraction of the world's potential. My heart may yet purr, or the coiled snake of vitality that lurks at my tailbone may shoot up and bite my brain. Protestants tend to delegate miracles to history or to one particular man, but I'm reluctant to presume I know God so well. This very morning, some sacred force may be buffeting the resistant walls of the present in hopes of defying nature.

I shudder at the thought. Stu Anderson, a physicist friend of mine, believes that the world in its substantial and finite physicality *is* conclusion, and what is born here dies here in a closed circle of existence. He sits in church on Sunday mornings, looking around the sanctuary as the congregation offers up prayers and says to himself, "*This is it*; this is God." Mystery ends at the physical boundaries of the created world. To a physicist entranced by the inordinate order of things, the universe's predictability is worthy of worship. My friend loves gravity. When he eats the bread and wine, they pass through his gullet in the same direction everything falls—toward the center of the spinning earth. This fact alone brings him to his knees.

Meanwhile, I sit in a pew across the aisle. I love the story of Pentecost, how "a sound came from heaven like the rush of a mighty wind" and the Holy Spirit descended on the followers of Jesus in tongues of flame. In a room full of men overcome by their God, I imagine an ordinary man with a quickening pulse. His thoughts blur and his mouth quivers as he speaks a language he does not know. The maelstrom of praise sweeping through the room fills his spirit to bursting. I relish the audacity of this story, how it is told with such confidence that twenty centuries of Christians, myself included, have believed it as fact. I love the idea of a magical God who can swoop into a room and set people's minds on fire.

I love the stories, but when it comes down to brass tacks, miracles make me nervous. Would the Great Magician ever pull a rabbit out of my hat? Would I even want it? With the exception of the mystics and martyrs among us (whose desire to commune with God surpasses all else), most people's feelings regarding the disruption of natural order are conflicted. We want healing but doubt we could survive that much love. Were God to leap from the woodwork, we'd flee in terror. Yet we long for it to be otherwise—for the external force governing the universe to intervene suddenly and set things straight. Stu theorizes that our need for hope is so strong we're willing to suspend common sense, all evidence to the contrary. For some reason, the bare facts we're given aren't enough for most of us. We must believe, with Emily Dickinson, that "A species stands beyond / Invisible as music / But positive as sound." We hold out hope, all the while assuming we will die without feeling God's bare hand.

What happens, then, when a biological tempest blows us inside out?

"The unpredictable can be detected only against a vast backdrop of predictability," Stu writes to me. Because I'm not a scientist, I doubt our ability to distinguish the unpredictable. Flames of spirit leaping from our crowns may well be part of the natural order of things. The kundalini coil may be waiting to spring into spiritual ecstasy within each of us. In other words, Jesus' healing the sick and raising the dead may not be miracles in the abracadabra sense, but rather a predictable possibility of which each one of us is capable—miracle embedded in matter; God dwelling in our cells. I need the story of Pentecost to remind me of what the apostles knew, that inspiration and connection across gulfs of language and a rapturous, communal unity are part of the human experience. The invisible music stands beyond our perception, but not beyond creation. When I take Communion, I kneel at the cusp of this conclusion. The bread may be yeast and flour or God's body. The wine may be heaven in a cup.

In the end I worship neither the intricate, definitive laws by which the world is governed nor a God who can defy creation's order with one sweeping hand. I worship the sly creative force that inhabits form and lets matter have its way. "We simply do not live in a world where God turns gravity off once in a while just to keep us hopping," Stu cautions. It's true. The restless wind is a piece in the fabric of predictability. We can rely on it to surprise us.

I extract my right arm from under the covers to scratch between Rhia's ears, more for my own comfort than hers. She's four years old and still rambunctious. For the rest of the day, she'll rip around the house, skidding recklessly across the wood floor and tangling herself inside rumpled throw rugs. Petting will not be permitted. The ozone in the air will make Rhia crazy; it will unleash that wildness lying dormant under her domesticity. Now is my only opportunity to receive her sleepy affection.

Finally I heave myself out of bed. When I retrieve the newspaper from the front steps (it's heavy and wet inside its plastic bag), I see that the wind has blown one of my porch screens out of its frame and onto the lawn. The porch feels vulnerable without it. Before the morning is over it will only get worse; my job today is to take down the front screen door, strip the peeling paint, give it a fresh coat of white, and replace the torn screen. I've been saving this project for a day with weather so miserable I won't mind spending hours in the basement. This is it. With a hammer, screwdriver, and lubricant I battle the pegs out of their rusty hinges. Once I lift the door from its frame, the hole gapes. Over the next few days, as coats of paint dry in the basement, the papergirl will aim the *Star Tribune* over the threshold and a ruddy house finch will give serious consideration to nesting among some vines I've hung inside. I find myself slightly embarrassed for my house. Its weaknesses are aired. I can no longer control what enters.

My exposed house reminds me of a rare poetic moment I walked into once when I was a teenager. The high school I attended was at the top of a hill overlooking Tarrytown, with its steepled churches, stacks of houses, and the Hudson River, steely and broad. Unlike the majority of American schools built in the past fifty years, Sleepy Hollow High was generous with its windows. Two full wings faced the river with enormous panes of Plexiglas. From the social studies and English classrooms, I could watch barges chug northward and seagulls circle over the town. Beyond the classrooms with views, the school spread uphill in a series of enclosed courtyards. Every hallway was bordered on one side by classrooms and the other by windows looking inward. Shortcuts between wings of the school passed diagonally across lawns and under a few trees.

On that particular June afternoon, both chemistry class and the school day were almost over. From our Bunsen burners we watched the gray sky sink lower and the wind suddenly flail the gnarled cedar against the window. Electricity in the atmosphere entered our bodies, already static with end-of-the-school-year energy. The bell rang. We were let loose the same time as the skies. Rain came sideways off the river, beating against the hall windows and streaking in open doors. When thunder struck, the crowded corridors screamed. The students, unrestrained, ran. No teachers stepped forward to shut off the courtyards. I stood for a moment in an open doorway, books held behind me. My peers streamed past. The courtyard was obscured by rain; not even the opposite hallway was visible. I thought to myself, "Now *this* is education"—a school open to the elements, a storm raging into our lives. Half drenched, I joined the bodies flooding the hallway. There was animal blood in our veins.

It's an illusion, even with the screen door up, that I have any control over what enters my porch. The only protection the door offers me is visual; there's no lock and, if there was, a razor blade swipe would allow entrance. All it takes is a steel fist to break into my first-floor windows (as I learned the hard way) or a tornado to lift off my roof and deposit it across town (as I hope I'll never learn). The elements that demand entrance will have it. This is the order of the world. Beyond care and common sense, there's not a blessed thing I can do.

The same is true of our bodies. There's that charged moment before lightning strikes when breath comes short, hair suddenly thickens, and skin tightens with anticipation. Or when thunder unsettles the ground and our very bones leap from their joints. When Zeus took the form of a swan and alighted on Leda's mortal, white belly, undoubtedly he assumed rape was as much his domain as thrusting bolts of lightning from the sky. A virgin birth isn't so different. According to the Bible, sheer spirit, with an impulse and movement entirely its own, can interact with our embodied selves. It speaks in a booming voice ("Thus says the Lord!") and it laps at our brains like tongues of fire. That day in high school the storm taught me that concoctions cooked up in test tubes are small potatoes compared with the Real World, its unbidden force blowing into the halls. And this will always be the case. Even if we can explain it, predict it, and measure it, we can't control what's wild. Without any effort on my part, my lungs continue to take in air. They expand, filling my chest, and contract, whether I desire breath or not.

It's easy to attribute to God all that we consider a mystery. Over time, however, the boundary between what we dismiss as earthly and what we revere as divine has moved, calling into question a definition of God that relies on absence rather than substance. A solar eclipse no longer scares us into offering burnt sacrifices. Cloned sheep graze the pastures and babies are conceived in test tubes, making creation, if not less miraculous, at least more within human capacity. I heard a story about a Liberian woman living in Minnesota whose mother traveled from her remote village to visit for the first time. After a few days of vacation the woman went back to work, leaving her mother alone in the apartment. When she returned, she found her mother sitting on the front steps, refusing to go inside. "There's ghosts talking in there," she said. Only later did the daughter discover that the ghosts spoke through the answering machine. These days it's the intricate workings of dreams that send us racing from the house; it's fleeting moments of déjà vu, the origin of the big bang, and the intuitive connections between creatures and the land that fill us with awe. If it's wondrous and beyond our ken, we still chalk it up to God.

It's equally easy to dismiss as mundane those things we understand. When was the last time you were stunned by a machine's capacity to record the human voice? We draw up blueprints for a house or meteorological maps to predict incoming weather, and then the bungalow that's built or the storm that rattles its windows is too *obvious* to contain divinity. God is beyond the Beyond. Little Rhia, desperate to explore the doorless porch, is just a cat and can't possibly be a sacred presence. My threshold is just a threshold, with its peeling paint. We tend to disassociate God from what we know.

Surely there's a middle ground. I hang out with the physicist at church in hopes that his awe of the obvious will rub off on me. The more he understands the world, the more it merits his reverence. Looking at our congregation, he sees the potential for sacred presence not beyond ourselves but here, within us. Our blood, breath, and bones and the predictable way they work are enough to give us hope. Why look to the supernatural for answers when our own capacity for good is so great?

In exchange, I teach Stu the trouble with disbelieving in miracles. First of all, the realm of what we don't understand expands at the same rate as the universe. If we call the mysterious miraculous, then miracles may change but will always exist. Second, you never know when, with a sudden stirring of air, the electrons within you will leap from their orbits. It could happen tonight. It could happen at the moment of death, when there's no turning back to tell the scientists otherwise.

Down in the basement, I set up the door on sawhorses and pry off the frame that holds down the screen. Rusty staples line the underside; I lever them off with a screwdriver. When the screen is removed, the door is not much more than a few flimsy one-bytwos loosely held together by crossbars. Still, it takes me all morning to scrape the chipping white paint, sand down the rough spots, and give it a layer of primer. There's a bare lightbulb over my head. Rhia scampers around chasing dust motes and spiders, then finds a box of Styrofoam peanuts and settles inside it, the cardboard flaps pressing at her ears. In the basement window well, brilliant green ferns are whipped and soaked with rain. I feel busy in the hull of a ship, oblivious to the mounting waves.

I don't relish household jobs that require more than an hour of attention. I prime the slats impatiently, dipping the brush into thick white and spreading it over bare wood. I've bought a new screen that I will unroll from its tube, stretch tight across the frame, press into the little crevice and staple down, all for the sake of warding off insects. Is it worth it? But this door that is barely a door intrigues me. It permits me a room that's half inside and half out, like the airlock on a spaceship where astronauts transition from the void back into oxygen. Rain blows in and rots the red oil–painted floorboards of the threshold, but my door screens out the larger forces of urbanized nature: the alley cats, hulking raccoons, the squirrels that skitter up the evergreen in heedless frenzy. My porch is a halfway house for spirit, a place where I can welcome the wild on my own terms. I want it to be an inviting place. Fresh paint is important.

In Celtic mythology, "thin places" are those where the visible and invisible worlds touch—where light and land, story and a history of reverence all converge to weaken physicality's resistance to the ineffable. At the summer solstice, the sun pierces the single, tunneled entrance to a grave mound and illuminates its altar stone. The stand of old growth sets its roots so deep into the earth and its branches so near the clouds that, standing in their midst, your soul is startled into praise. I've watched a storm cross Lake Superior, the phalanx of black pushing back a blue sky, rain angling forward, and found myself splayed wide and receptive by the seeming boundlessness of this fresh water, my roiling surface open to the oncoming fury. Surely there are places in the landscape where the vibrant essence of things springs out from matter and we *touch metal*. James Joyce called it epiphany: "When something's soul, its whatness, leaps to us from the vestment of its appearance."

But that whatness resides outside of ourselves only in part. I've also been to thin places—Chartres Cathedral, Stonehenge, the Chinese Temple of Heaven; holy places, certainly, full of potential for epiphany—and not felt a blessed thing except, at most, the pulse of privilege and awe. I'm weary from walking so far. I'm hungry, or I need to find a bathroom. I can see holiness without crossing over into the raw experience of it. In fact, this is most commonly the case. Whatever convergence of outward arrival and inward receptivity is necessary to experience mystery, it can't be brewed in a test tube. Revelation simply happens. Even my physicist friend can't recreate the conditions of his moment of insight—"This is it!"—when God fused Godself to the physical world in defiance of Stu's Lutheran heritage. Perhaps the whatness leaps up from matter all the time. It's when our own whatness leaps to meet it (as it did during that rainy moment in my high school hallway) that epiphany happens.

As the paint dries, I sweep up rusty staples and wonder—if my porch is the thin place in my house, what is its equivalent in my body? The eyes, with their transparent skin and seeming depth? The soft space of sex, where sensation reaches up unexpectedly to my core? Or is it more like sleep, when the body leans into that place of rest and the unfathomable working of the inner life unfurls itself in memories, dreams, and the streamlined rushing of wind? It could be as close as my lungs, taking breath from the atmosphere (my chest's tremendous capacity for air! Every two seconds the storm blows in and out) and releasing it without so much as a thought. Perhaps this thin place resides in me and I can enter it as I enter my porch later on, carelessly passing through to retrieve the mail or intentionally sitting out there in the evening, lighting a candle and smelling the washed earth, the birth scent of worms and the night air as it stirs the city. Perhaps we are made of thin places. Even the thick skin of my feet is porous.

There's no explaining why wind whipped through my body that night and knocked out my metaphoric screens, why it chose that moment to lift my roof and set me down askew on what I thought was familiar territory. I know less now than ever. Belief and disbelief were easy enough before physical sensation made them seem irrelevant and somehow antiquated. The world will go its merry way despite any construct I create to understand it. Carl Jung reportedly said that if someone claims they've seen God, all you can do is nod your head. I find myself nodding in the basement, nodding to Rhia asleep in her box, nodding to myself, because it's all I can do. Irrefutable experience contains miracle enough to render me speechless.

I wash my hands and climb upstairs. Out on the porch, the wind has died down and moisture hangs heavy in the air. I retrieve an errant window screen from the lawn, fit it into its frame, and note that its latch is missing—another project, another run to the hardware store. The porch still feels unprotected without its screen door, but also receptive, welcoming, not a bad place for a house finch to nest. I stand on the threshold, hands pressed against the rain-dampened frame the way I can't when the door is up, teetering between the world I love and the mystery I long to touch. Perhaps the thin place within me is this invitation I extend daily to what's inexplicable and wild—to the spirit, the wily wind, that seeps through my screens and suppositions and cells and is ever opening me wide.

Ah, Poor Bird

Evelyn was on her knees under the bridal spirea, planting pink impatiens, when a tiny thrashing in the grass caught her attention. She called out in a panicky voice. I dropped my trowel and bent beside her to see. The bird wasn't long from the egg, pale skin pulled over bulbous, dark eyes, wings like flailing arms, its beak unformed and shockingly yellow. When I touched it with my gardening glove, it opened its mouth desperately.

"What are we going to do?" Evelyn asked.

I looked around for a nest, but there was none. "It's going to die," I said. "It might be best to kill it now."

Evelyn fluttered. She wouldn't touch it.

The bird thrust its wings into the sod and its beak in the air. Its head rotated frantically. "I'll do it," I said, and picked it up between finger and thumb. Even through my glove I could feel its weightless bones held tight with translucent skin. When I placed the bird in one of Evelyn's seedling containers, it pushed its feet and rubbed its face against the plastic.

But I couldn't. In back of the compost, I found a sheltered spot among the daylilies where I couldn't bring myself to snap that tiny, straining neck. I left it in misery.

All afternoon, shame lurked around the edges of my work. Was it commitment to nonviolent living that made me inhumane? Or simply cowardice? I was afraid of compassion that requires killing. Even more, I was afraid of beautiful bones cracking between my fingers and that instant where life leaves a body. I finished gardening, made dinner, and washed the dishes, all the while resigning myself to this weakness in my character. I prayed for the baby bird's swift and natural death. When I emptied the dinner compost, I peeked behind the arch of daylily leaves and there the bird was, still thrusting helplessly against the earth, straining toward me for food. I couldn't bear it. I filled the compost bucket at the hose and, with my naked hands, held the bird under water, held its writhing bones—it strained toward the air!—held it while tears stung my cheeks because I despise love like this that takes us into death. I want to turn my face from merciless nature. I want to run. I don't understand a world that requires of me what I most hate, while the cardinal in the elm above me sings cheerily. My own song is this bird's burial, and the most I can give:

Ah, poor bird! Take thy flight!
High above the sorrow of this sad night.

On Sunday Morning

ON SUNDAY MORNING I throw on a sweater and a pair of jeans, hop in the car, and drive the river road north toward the Witch's Hat, a stone water tower perched at the Twin Cities' highest elevation. You can see its green-tiled, pointy hat from almost anyplace in southeast Minneapolis, like a pagan response to the steeple-dominant St. Paul. My church (with no steeple; in fact, barely looking like a church) sits at the tower's foot. The tower is a lightning rod for the congregation's affection. When we drive down the highway or look out from hospital windows or walk the Franklin Avenue bridge, we see the tower and think fondly of one another.

Inside the sanctuary, I shake the greeter's hand and slip into my pew, center left. Its occupants refer to Christians in the third person (as in "Christians are obsessive!"). And when we sing "This Little Light of Mine," we dance our pointer fingers like happy candles. During the sermon we braid hymnal ribbons, pass notes scribbled with pew pencils on bulletin margins, and don't allow a platitude to pass without wry comment. We are Christian through and through, born, baptized, and bred, and the implications of this inheritance make us squirm. We cluster together to revel in irreverence or, perhaps more honestly, to find company in our discomfort.

I've positioned myself to have a good time in church—far enough forward to see the kids' faces during the children's sermon, far enough back that the pastor won't notice my pew's misdemeanors. Behind me sits the Jiménez family; Sam is four and will spend the entire service running to the children's corner and back with piles of Berenstain Bear books. He flips the pages in a great hurry. If the service grows irksome or stale, I borrow Sam's reading material or his Etch A Sketch.

Even so, as I take my seat each Sunday I wonder again, *Why am I here?* The organist blasts out a prelude, the come-lately congregation slips in during the call to worship, and, with one glance at the bulletin, I know the language we'll use to praise our maker won't be worth the poor-quality paper it's printed on. There are plenty of good reasons to leave the United Methodist Church— its sanctification of patriarchy, its institutionalized fear of nature, its prejudice against sexual minorities, and the way it systematically stymies spiritual growth for the sake of conformity—to name a few. I respect those who leave in protest. Surely their souls are better for being unsaved.

In the meantime, I find myself magnetized, almost against my will, to the Witch's Hat tower, to this church, and into this unruly pew. In spite of our denomination's rampant imperfections, my particular congregation fights for low-income housing and marches in the Gay Pride parade; it sends health care and construction workers overseas; it debates what it means to grow in faith and be a prophetic voice in an urban community. On Father's Day, a Dixieland jazz band provides the music. On Maundy Thursday, the women gather in an upper room to wash one another's feet. During the denomination's general conference, we send a van of laypeople to protest discriminatory policies. I know of few churches as suited to my feminist, activist leanings. With a candle on the altar this community still honors a six-year-old who died twenty years ago. After I lost my possessions in the fire, these people clothed me, and even now they recognize the sweater or shoes I am wearing with a smile. How can I reconcile my love for this rare bird—a healthy, radical, spiritual community—with the institution's hypocrisy and the drudgery of Sunday worship?

Our first hymn is "Stand Up, Stand Up for Jesus." I stand up, but some don't. Enough members of the congregation sing boldly and our organist is accomplished enough that I survive this hymn the way I survive most—by singing its spirit rather than the words. "From victory unto victory his army shall he lead, 'til every foe is vanquished and Christ is Lord indeed." The militarism and "Praise Jesus!" mentality make me crazy if I pay too close attention. By singing, do I perpetuate this ridiculous ideology? Instead I've convinced myself that the words are vehicles for the sacred language of music, Sharon droning alto beside me, Mary in front wavering the melody, elderly Charles Strom across the aisle belting out the bass, voices rallied by a blood-pumping tune into a musical unity that can dispel content. This is always the battle I fight in church—slashing through religious trappings in hopes of finding spirit.

Early in the service (too early for my tastes), we enter into a time of communal Joys and Concerns, sharing our prayers that we might uphold one another over the coming week, and every Sunday we roll our eyes when Edith Halloway stands up. Edith wears T-shirts with too many stains; her hair is in disheveled pigtails. When she opens her mouth, another fraction of her one eternal run-on sentence emerges: "Bus fees are going up, you know, and I think we need to help those poor souls down at

Glenwood Housing, and the last time I got a transfer . . ." Without fail she offends someone, usually a person of color. Still, I like how prayer gets offered up in this place. Once a man whose mother died began his prayer with, "So a rabbi, a priest, and a Methodist pastor walked into a bar" and ended in tears. And once a woman screamed at God: "How *dare* you let Jerry die so young!" More often people lift up the ordinary touchstones—birthdays, illness, transitions, urban crises, world events. The pastor, speechless in the face of our complex lives, retreats into formula. None of us knows how to pray, really. We flounder together, trying.

I used to say that church did nothing to feed me spiritually, that I went for coffee hour, the social life. My pew mates are lively lunch companions, making Scandinavian critiques of the sermon (too much emotion) or the potluck hot dishes (too much spice). The congregation practices a contemporary version of barn raising, auctioning off our sweat equity then turning out in droves to paint houses, build retaining walls, or, in my case, dig a new driveway and raise trellises. Over the years, the small group of women that gathers to celebrate the winter solstice has howled our pain and lit candles in hope, from which lasting friendships have emerged. I value the opportunity on Sundays to play with the kids, fulfilling my commitment to them at their baptism and my own childless need to engage those with broader imaginations than my own. This church provides community in an otherwise disconnected world. Is that reason enough to remain Christian?

It is Joys and Concerns, though, and our fumbling attempts to translate longing into prayer, that teaches me how essential community is to the life of the spirit. Over the years, these people have rejoiced at my coming out bisexual, lit candles for my infant nephew who died of SIDS, prayed me through depression, and witnessed my anger at church polity and our nation's aggressive egotism. Likewise I have shared in their stunning, artless prayers. Joys and Concerns binds my particular journey to one larger and more corporate, capable of greater influence (for good or ill) than anything I'd muster alone. I am connected and accountable; here my spiritual ramblings are spun into the frayed cord of humanity, ever lengthening our presence in the world.

At least that's what I glimpse in rare moments, when I'm not distracted by Edith's rants or the pastor's inadequacies. We respond to Joys and Concerns, all our agony and longing sent Godward, with silence. Luckily the pastor composes her final prayer in that moment, so the duration of quiet is substantial. Our pleas are palpable then, moving in the churned air between the tops of our heads and the rafters. We take a unitive breath. Our shoulders sink. The entire scope of my being, it seems, slides through that slight aperture of quiet.

Then we end with the Lord's Prayer, using "Our Creator" instead of "Our Father" but otherwise sticking to the old version, asking forgiveness for "trespasses" rather than "sins," and seeking to avoid "temptation" rather than the gentler "time of trial." Mentally I bring "heaven" down from the skies and disperse it through millions of molecules; I drop the g from kingdom, asking instead for familial closeness. With these revisions, my affection for this prayer is able to run backward in time, through my childhood recitations and centuries of Christian worship to the abbreviated version Jesus taught the disciples; it sweeps across the present in this familiar chorus of devotion. I love the first exhalation after "amen," when the words dissolve and we return to our separate bodies, stiff in the pews.

The children's sermon, while lively, always revolves around the wearisome theme of God's abiding love. The choir is spirited in an off-key, overly enthusiastic way. I could do without the adult sermon. My reverence for clergy is minimal (aren't we all ordained?), and it galls me that one person's Bible interpretation serves as the focal point for worship rather than, say, silence or creative expression. But there are those who adore the sermons and grudgingly endure Joys and Concerns. Community is nothing if not compromise. By sitting through a service, I learn that there are no absolutes regarding what nurtures people's spirits. Certainly you can choose a house of worship more befitting your temperament, but eventually any service becomes a potluck of elements that do or don't appeal to your palate. What matters is whether, by the time you reach the percolating pot of cheap church coffee, you've somehow been fed.

One morning, in the middle of the sermon, the congregation's attention was drawn down from the pulpit to a tiny hand that rose from behind the solid wood altar rail. A four-year-old finger traced the altar's carved lettering: "DO THIS IN REMEMBRANCE OF ME." Her hand, disconnected from a body, was entrancing—a dancing sea anemone, full of more grace than the preacher's words droning above her. The entire congregation saw it (a silent, rippled laughter passed over us), and no one stopped her. Her M's slow jig, the C's sweep, the final trinity of parallel lines, engraved in me the import of communal remembrance. *You are gathered to honor what is holy. Do this, so you do not forget.*

Awash in cynicism and impatience, I must work hard not to forget. The compromises that are fundamental to forming community, any community, eventually also compromise our principles—thus the United Methodist Church, in its attempts at unity, backs policies of exclusion; thus no liturgy is ultimately, inclusively satisfying. When faced with such a grim reality, most people these days forsake institutionalized religion. Who has the forbearance for nickering committee work, for whitewashed ritual, for crazy women who prattle offensively during Joys and Concerns? The fact that I am here is more a testament to stubbornness than faith. I want to believe in community. I want the connective tissue of religion to bind disparate lives together where so little else does. This is my private folly.

But then at church I find my folly not so private. After the pastor extends an invitation to Communion, Barb Strom (a retired physical therapist, spry and bright) hurries to the front. Barb is the first in line, first to kneel, and first to return to her pew. I never noticed this until she shared why in an adult education conversation. "Eating the bread and grape juice doesn't do it all for me," Barb told us, without regret. "I get that part out of the way. What I like is watching each person in the congregation slowly come down the center. That's why I sit near the aisle—so I can see your faces. I spend that time praying for each of you. You're my church family. Communion for me is about sharing a meal with you, being grateful for each of you."

Now the pastor breaks a chunk from the loaf; now she says my name, "The bread of life, given for you." I dip the grainy crust in the cup and kneel at the rail, as my parents and grandparents always have; I pause over the Eucharist as Christians do, across time and tradition; I eat as every being eats, only now I'm remembering this and giving thanks. My reason for partaking in Communion is not what church doctrine would dictate, nor perhaps Jesus himself. Barb has let these go and, over time, taught me to do the same. Or rather, I have allowed interpretations of the ritual to layer themselves with what matters most to me—a moment of shared attention focused on mystery. For me, for now, this is enough.

Back in the pew, I sing the remaining Communion hymns while the rest of the congregation filters forward. At its core, the Christian faith calls people not to *believe* so much as to *participate*—in healing one another, working for justice, deepening relationships, and honoring the spirit that lends us life. I cannot let go of church nor my tradition as long as I value these. We join in our final hymn and remain standing for the pastor's well-chosen benediction, from John Howell:

> Like a rock, God is under our feet.
> Like a roof, God is over our heads.
> Like the horizon, God is beyond us.
> Like water in a pitcher, God is within us and in the pouring out
> of us.
> Like a pebble in the sea, we are in God.
> Let us go out and change our world as God has changed
> our lives.

These words would be a welcome end to our morning except that announcements follow—what petitions need signing, who's performing in concert, when the youth are leaving for the amusement park, and don't forget to make a sandwich for the homeless shelter on your way out. Our leg muscles twitch; we glance at the clock. All the while holiness rises in and through and between us, rises eagerly with our bodies, and, in greeting, extends its hand.

More Poor Birds

"REMEMBER THAT BABY BIRD?" Evelyn asks me from her side of the picket fence. A month has passed since I performed my first mercy killing. Evelyn's impatiens are now heaps of pink and white.

"Sure," I say, rising from my knees and peeling off my garden gloves. "I even wrote a little essay about it. I should let you read it sometime." I wipe my hands on my jeans. "I ended up drowning it. It was horrible."

But Evelyn doesn't want to listen. "I found another one this morning," she tells me. "It fell out of the birdhouse. I put it back in the nest and I think it's okay." She's flushed and looks almost victorious.

I'm relieved; I don't want to raise my courage again to the demands of cruel compassion. I can still see the bird's unopened eyes and eager mouth. "That's great," I say.

"Isn't it ironic that people get so upset about killing baby birds and don't have a problem with aborting fetuses?" Evelyn asks. The sun is out, Evelyn's geraniums glow scarlet, and it takes me a moment to register her sudden shift in subject. *People? Fetuses?* I have an instant to decide whether I will address the not-so-subtle insult or launch into the abortion debate or avoid this conflict by ignoring my neighbor's bizarrely inaccurate comparison. A wave of nausea passes over me. Compassion can require cruelty, and Evelyn, with evangelical conviction, must press the human corollary into my consciousness. My friends who have gone through abortion found it elemental and wrenching. I can barely grasp what they teach me, that ending the life of a being, not yet a child, can be an act of love. Baffled, I'm unable to frame my thoughts into an adequate response. Evelyn nervously changes the subject: weeds and their overabundance in our gardens. She thinks I'm offended when, really, I'm not. I'm just busy making myself a promise—that the next time Evelyn finds a nestless baby bird in her grass and needs a mercy killer, she's on her own.

Swimming Outside the Lines

THIS SUMMER, MY FRIEND JIMMY and I determine, we will swim—we will plunge into city lakes and crawl wide circles under a sweltering sky.

So when that first sweaty day arrives we head to Cedar Lake, one among ten thousand and the cleanest inside the metro area. It is Saturday; everyone in Minnesota, I imagine, is pulling on a bathing suit and hightailing it to water. Jimmy and I take a wooded trail down to the lake. Across the way is the official beach, all yellow and shimmering, and around the bend is the crowded, unofficial one, where adults with dreadlocks linger in mudflats and teenagers smoke weed. We forgo both beaches for a random, solitary spot; we hang our towels from a log and run in, shouting, the reeds bending before us. Soon we're in over our heads. Jimmy is a state high school champion swimmer, long distance, and I can swim for miles, so we begin circumnavigating the lake, arms pumping, legs thrashing, the cool air filling our lungs. The flags of our towels are far behind. To the north, Minneapolis rises like a make-believe city. Our bodies propel us halfway around the lake; we are powerful, exhilarated, free. The lake holds us in its dark palm.

Fifty yards from the city beach, we stop to catch our breath. Treading water, Jimmy and I give each other high fives, our day is so fine.

A man in a metal fishing boat buzzes his way toward us, wearing an orange life jacket and frowning at our bobbing heads. "Hey!" he calls to us, skidding the boat sideways and cutting the motor. "You're not allowed to swim outside the designated area."

"What?!" I answer, incredulous. Across the lake, someone jumps off a log near the mudflats, and the splash carries over the surface. "You've got to be kidding." I'm confounded; are the artificial boundaries that divide up land now enforced on lakes too? Forty square feet are roped off at the official beach, where some kids have plastic bubbles around their forearms and others do handstands, waving pale feet in the air. A lifeguard peers down from his white tower, which is a good thing for the kids. But does the city of Minneapolis really expect Jimmy and me to clip our strokes to fit within that confinement?

"I don't get it," I say, stubbornly. "Can't we be responsible for ourselves?"

"Nope," he says. Now I can see the badge on his life jacket, and the City of Lakes logo on his cap. "What if someone on shore thought you were drowning and called 911? You'd have to pay the expense. It's for your own good."

I fume and pedal my feet.

"You have to get out," he says.

"Our car's on the other side," Jimmy points. "We can't walk around."

This irks him. "I'll give you a ride then. Wait here." And he pulls the starter, swinging the boat around toward the marsh, where two swimmers are doing the breast stroke. Blue exhaust fills our lungs.

Incredulous, Jimmy and I dog-paddle toward shore, exchanging epithets about the swimming police. We can't believe it's this man's job to troll Cedar Lake all summer, rounding up triathletes and long-distance swimmers. "Just think of the thousands of Minnesotans swimming right now," I say to Jimmy. "Isn't it pointless to try stopping them?" More than that, I consider the human instinct for freedom, especially outside on a summer day, and how quickly our society's obsession with safety and responsibility becomes constricting. Jimmy and I brainstorm alternative ways the city could express its genuine concern for our welfare: swimming licenses or designated long-distance lakes. Or signs declaring, Swim at Your Own Risk. It wouldn't take much.

"What's he doing?" I ask, my feet sinking into the silty bottom. The boat is a speck over by the mudflats; it shows no intention of picking us up.

"Jerking us around," Jimmy says. In his activism work, Jimmy has frequent encounters with the law, resulting in a resounding skepticism toward authority. He tells me about being arrested outside the Federal Building after protesting our government's support of Israeli aggression. "The police did their job routinely, but then the sheriff at the jail pretended to get all tied up in paperwork. We didn't get let out until two in the morning. They were just stalling to show us who was in charge." The motorboat creeps along the opposite shore heading south. By this point, we could have swum the distance. The lake glints, wind lassoing its surface. We shiver in the shallows.

I wonder if our swimming cop or the city council members who made this rule have ever swum across a lake. I wonder if they know pumping strength, lungs tight with air, muscles sleek and straining atop a body of water. Because once you know wet elation, there's no erasing it. A turbulent force seeps into your pores. The arbitrary restrictions of those who feel responsible are

like red, bouncing buoys sectioning off the surface, while underneath, the lake roils. Dipping into anything that free entails risk.

Half an hour later, the man zips over and we climb aboard.
He gives us life preservers and launches into a lecture on rule
obedience. We speed across the lake, hot wind lapping at wet
skin. As we pass the illegal beach, our escort winces and defends
himself: "We're working to get that place shut down." Jimmy and
I are no longer interested. We point out our towels on the shore
and, once the boat is idling, vault over its side. The cop har-
rumphs, glad to be rid of us. The silent backs we turn to him are
indomitable, and clean.

Royal We

*I*N ITS USUAL STATE, the Mississippi curves surreptitiously through the city, tucked between steep slopes, muddy, sluggish, with hardly a ripple marring its surface. I have thought the river lacked conviction and grown impatient with its indirect twisting; I've wanted to say, *Get on with being a river!* and bang my fists against the Army Corps of Engineers' tall chain-link fences. The thick, mild-mannered current flows at a beleaguered pace. Those of us residing in the Twin Cities go about our lives without ever descending to the level of the river's scummy surface. We cross the gorge with the assumption that the river knows its place— that its identity is well contained between banks far below us.

But last April the Mississippi returned to its frothed and un-tamed state, overflowing banks, saturating soil, and asserting a frenzied presence on the landscape. A wicked winter had caused rivers all over the state (the Red River, the Minnesota, the Snake, the Rum) to run high. The mayor of Grand Forks remarked with distress that disaster shouldn't strike so soon after the flood of '97.

The newspaper was filled with photos of townspeople in winding lines passing sandbags down toward furious waters. The St. Paul waterfront (parking ramps, city streets) flooded. The Minneapolis River Road was closed. Ducks swam between trees at Hidden Falls Park. Traveling anywhere in the state involved detours.

One afternoon, I descended the hill from the university to the barricaded road with my friend Jorge, who monitors water quality for pleasure and wanted me to see the Mississippi's flood stage up close. There is a low wall between the river and the bike path, but that day the path was flooded; simmering whorls on the surface revealed water still coming in. The newscasters were predicting another week before the crest hit the cities; the cement wall would soon be under water. Already the low parts of the road were impassable.

Jorge and I found a steep, grassy slope and sat down to watch the river pass at a dizzying speed. Not a quarter mile upstream was St. Anthony Falls with its brawling, heart-stopping roar. Foam sped by in shifting formations; huge, uprooted trees spun recklessly, effortlessly; the surface seemed to leap ahead of itself in the great rush downriver. Jorge and I speculated that a race between a running human and a log would be won by the log. We cheered the river on, shouting, "You go, girl!" and "Strut your stuff!"

The Mississippi was on the move, and for the first time since I'd made its acquaintance fourteen years ago, I was exhilarated by its personality. Jorge and I rolled up our jeans, removed socks and shoes, and continued our walk upriver along a street usually busy with traffic. Our feet were numb before we had a chance to suck in air. The river was biting, rebellious. The real Mississippi was finally lashing out at the world, thrusting its might, its chunks of ice and uprooted trees against bridge pilings and our meager blockades. Over the next week, as the river rose and crested—as it spilled over the retaining wall at Bohemian Flats, as flood plains around the state filled and the

Corps opened locks to manage the flow—Jorge and I checked it daily; we memorized light posts as measurements of depth and we studied the channel's seething wrath. Here was a river asserting itself on the landscape, finally touching all the places it *could* touch and wielding influence, shedding its silty nutrients over tended lawns, through wooded parks, into farmers' fields and across city streets from Lake Itasca down through the bayous of New Orleans in one slow, stumbling wave. Finally the river showed spunk. I want to remember how effortlessly a river forsakes its banks and takes hold of the land in a clenching, icy grip.

Who am I? Most of my days I spend under the impression that who I am exists within walls of skin. Personhood contains identity. When I use the word "myself" I mean this creature of guilty determination, flightful imagination, nervous tics, many friends, a penchant for solitude, and a body at its peak—the person who is present when I step into the room. Recently, however, I've experienced the odd phenomenon of complete strangers approaching me with the assumption that they know me, simply because they have read something I have written. Without my awareness, I have whispered a story into their ear and unwittingly entered into relationship. I react to their overtures with awkward speechlessness. And so I've been forced to consider the possibility that selfhood floods, that it reaches beyond our perceived banks and sinks silt into the lives surrounding it. Perhaps identity is only partially contained. The rest seeps into the riverbed and in seasons past has sunk into the flatlands, for good or ill, of those whose lives border mine.

Yesterday I got a call from Frank, the former owner of my house. He was in Minneapolis to escape the Arizona heat and visit a friend. "How's the old homestead?" he asked.

house and my house were brothers; they lived in Evelyn's garage during 1934, while construction was under way. When the group from church helped me put in a driveway, we dug up a passel of marbles and a few old hard liquor bottles, their clear glass rippled and thick. I try to imagine the family who strung up the acres of clothesline in my yard and wonder where all of their kids must have slept. This has not always been a happy place; when Frank bought it, the floors had been used hard and the trunks of scrub trees had grown through a chain-link fence along the alley. According to the abstract, a woman was widowed here. Still, numerous New Age friends tell me my house has "good energy." While it's unclear to me what this means, I know the house's palpable welcome and that I'm more at ease here, more myself, than anywhere else. Perhaps I live with hospitable ghosts. Perhaps energy adds up to ambience and becomes the pulsing heart of a place.

As for my own molecules, I've mingled them with my home, apparently, within the minds of readers, and in the Mississippi River at its source near Lake Itasca. One fall a group of artists, musicians, and writers traveled to the headwaters for a working weekend; we spent a brilliant Saturday morning at the creek with our notebooks open, sketching children balancing on rocks, writing about the origin of rivers, and translating laughter and rushing water into musical scores. Pine woods skirted wetlands of cattails and wild rice. The creek was clear, cold, and ordinary. It seemed odd to me that this bend in its path, emerging from marsh and collecting itself into a celebrated trickle, should draw tourists from around the globe. The spot was lovely but hardly astonishing. Perhaps we were drawn here by this very humbleness. We knew how far this water would travel, how it would grow wide, murky, and magnificent, cutting through the continent, rambling among dells and cornfields, spreading out into the sim-

I told him about everything that had changed, the cherry tree my dad and I planted, the new stained glass window, how a work team from church helped me raise trellises against the back alley. "The paint is peeling in the bathroom," I told him. "My sister and I are going to redo it in August. It's kind of sad—the bathroom's the last remnant of your personality."

"Well," Frank said, "it's time." His voice was buoyant. Frank enjoys knowing that his house is well loved.

I described for him how the Engleman ivy has grown up the north side of the house and hangs in a swaying curtain across the bathroom window. "We're going to paint ivy creeping in the window, twining around the molding and getting all tangled on the tub. I want more nature in the house."

"That sounds perfect," Frank said. "Just like you."

The more I considered it, though, I would never dream of such a bold design had Frank not first painted the claw-foot toenails audacious red, and layered the green linoleum with white spirals. More than erasing evidence of Frank's influence, my ivy will continue in his tradition, adapting his freedom with the paintbrush to my own aesthetics. Personality gets layered onto a house, each successive owner covering over the past and yet indelibly marked by it. Frank's enduring impact is less on the bathroom walls than on me. I can recognize it because I know Frank; his style is primary and playful. But surely the choices of other previous owners (to paint the woodwork white, to allow the backdoor to buckle, not to enclose the porch) also exert their subtle agency on my house. How many cells that are not my own make up the ethos of home?

Fragments of my house's heritage have come to me, mostly through Evelyn's stories. An African-American man with AIDS spent his last years here before entering hospice care. One year a maple tree in the front yard was toppled by a windstorm and smashed in the front porch roof. The two men who built Evelyn's mering delta, and finally merging with salt and summer heat in the Gulf of Mexico. We weren't in Itasca for largess or conclusion. We were gathered for a small start, a trickle of anticipation.

An artist friend introduced me to the headwater ritual: set aside your notebook, roll up your jeans, and shuffle across the creek. Later, when you're standing on a bank by a wide and rumbling current, you can honestly claim to have walked across the Mississippi. "This way you also send your molecules on the most American of journeys," my friend explained.

Halfway across, pebbles between my toes, I imagined an unimpressive drip of sweat and a few shed flakes of ankle skin being whisked away, adding minuscule depth and width to the river. They'd swirl in eddies, churn under the engines of barges, and sweep past awareness into the ocean, where identity gets washed into a million heaving swells. Surely most of our presence in the world is invisible. After we send our molecules on their way, we rarely give them another thought except perhaps in our prayers, when we yearn to burst forth from our bodies into something broad, sweeping, and tidal.

I take my image of heaven not from Renaissance painters (angels lifted above the earth, their robes rustled by a celestial wind) but rather from *Star Trek,* a body of mythology more befitting my generation. In one episode, a shape-shifter has the opportunity to return home after being alienated from his people since birth. He arrives at the planet to find a glinting, mercurial sea—an ocean of his people, all restored to their natural liquid state. Standing on the shore, he melts with desire back into his origin. In this place is holy union, commingling, and communion, the primeval singularity from which all shape-shifters emerge and to which they return. Individuality seeps into common identity. As I imagine it, we don't lose self after death so much as become most fully who we are, wed like water to water with every other creature. Unitive and sweeping, the alpha and omega are ourselves beyond the confluence.

Meanwhile, on this side of the great divide, I dig my toes into the sand, skipping smooth stones of longing over what I cannot know.

It's not identity beyond the grave that interests me so much as who I am *now*. Still, the clues seem most evident after loss. A member of my congregation died recently—Leona Nelson, pillar of the community, a quiet woman who wore out the cushions on the eighth pew back, left side, with forty-five years of sitting. For the past decade of Sundays, I have sidled down the pew behind her and touched the sharp blade of her shoulder in greeting. She pivoted around to extend her thin hand. "How are you, dear?" She'd clasp mine and hold on. When my pew's inhabitants grew rowdy (during hymns about the blood of Jesus, for instance), Leona would lean back as though she wanted to be in on our joke and scold, "Now, you kids behave!" Occasionally she'd just wag her finger. Her memorial service was held on her eighty-seventh birthday. I slipped into my pew to find a cluster of roses and a beaming photograph of Leona on the seat in front of me. I missed her crackly voice.

My community grieves well, raging at God against our loss, singing with teary gusto, and telling story after story about the deceased until we've exhausted our memories and we're confident we'll remember for one another should anyone forget. At Leona's service, her peers recounted Leona's adventures in the WAVES, the women's division of naval reserves in World War II. Family and friends told of her commitment to healthful eating long before it was fashionable, and how she had tested children's recipes for Betty Crocker by recruiting congregation kids to cook. Her next-door neighbor told about Leona's wry, unabashed manner of suggesting he and his wife purchase curtains for their kitchen windows by giving them a book called *Cooking in the Nude*. We sang her favorite songs and listened to her grand-daughters' poetry. Afterward, down in the fellowship hall, I shared with Leona's daughter how Leona had come before me on the prayer chain. The phone would ring and Leona would say, "Hello, dear, I have some prayers for you"—very matter-of-fact, as though prayer came on the to-do list between grocery shopping and taking out the garbage.

There was an extravagant spread for lunch, including some of Leona's favorite recipes, and a back table filled with goodies baked from Betty Crocker's *Boys and Girls Cook Book*. When I saw the yellow spiral book propped on the table, with its familiar 1960s line drawings of children wearing oven mitts and stirring with their elbows in the air, I was amazed. I'd grown up with this cookbook, craving the castle-shaped birthday cake and canned pears made into bunny rabbits with cottage cheese tails. Suddenly I felt Leona's presence in a way I'd not known when she was alive—how she had touched my childhood halfway across the country, through deliberate lists of ingredients and the recipes she had coaxed children to cook. Long before I met Leona, my mother gripped the wooden spoon over my five-year-old fingers to stir cookie dough and Leona was there, hiding in the drafts that composed that moment. Suddenly it seemed any fraction of my past or cell of my body might not entirely be mine. I chose a Brownie Slowpoke, the recipe revised by a woman I'd prayed with, and baked by a neighbor who also cherished her; I sank my teeth through its layers of frosting and fudge as though it were the Eucharist, willingly taking into myself even more of the lives and loves of those surrounding me.

I usually understand our presence in one another's lives in terms of *influence*—a person's kindness or cruelty impacts others, the proverbial pebble dropped in a pond, concentric ripples circling out to the world. Then the pebble sinks, landing in a billow of muck, and begins its millennial transition into sand. When people influence me, part of them also takes up residence. In my grief after the twin towers of the World Trade Center collapsed, what came back to me was a memory of my red-necked, ninth grade social studies teacher during the Cold War. Mr. Pasierb stepped up to the classroom window and peered outside the building before instructing us that, when the commies bomb America, they'll target New York first. Even then I didn't buy into Pasierb's paranoid prejudice, but the fact of its existence was irrevocable and surfaces as often as I need to comprehend humanity's capacity for hatred. To say Pasierb influenced me (or Leona, or countless others, consciously or not) feels inadequate. Extrapolated conversations continue in my head long after our lives have parted. I rebel against, am inspired by, and, in some biological way, exist in relationship with people long after they have exited my life.

It's very well for my pastor to reassure her grieving congregation that Leona's spirit continues, residing in memory and welded to our being. But I want to travel backward to acknowledge that this has been true all along—for my past ten years of pew sitting, for thirty years of stirring with a wooden spoon—and that death is no prerequisite for another's spirit to indwell my being. Daily, I bump into my mother in me, her voice emerging from my throat when I sing those gusty hymns, her social fears manifest in my stilted posture. Or there's my father, reaching to shift gears with my right hand. I've absorbed my best teachers into the pause between asking a question and the first tentative student's response. And my friend's ritualistic whimsy at the Mississippi headwaters lodges like a stick against the current. If who I am contains so many others, then how much of myself floats about, beyond my control, for good or ill dropping its silt into the groundwater of our collective unconscious? I don't ask to call attention to how often and how deeply we impact one another; I ask to know, without delusion, the bounds of identity.

"Me" may be a false construct, a manner of holding tightly to my own smallness. I'm fond of the South African term *ubuntu*, as Desmond Tutu defines it: "A person is a person through other persons. Ubuntu means that my humanity is inextricably bound up in yours." How this uproots my independence, my very American concept of self! And yet without others to remember, interact with, make love to and be angry at—without community to contain my selfhood, I am loosely knit bones and a rattled head. Taken literally, God's great commandment, "Love your neighbor as yourself," challenges us to see our neighbor containing us and contained in us. Identity is fluid. We love neighbors through care for ourselves, and we love ourselves through the care of our neighbors. "Me," then, is an illusion of incarnation. Really we are a royal We, each one of us containing the whole of humanity.

Now it is July, 7:00 A.M., a Saturday. The river crested months ago and has retreated into summer lethargy. Jorge and I load the canoe on the car and drive up the Mississippi toward Bohemian Flats, a grassy plain and boat launch near the University of Minnesota. The river road is a creeping parade of similarly hatted automobiles, jaunty with anticipation of a peculiar urban adventure—the Great Mississippi River Canoe Run. Humidity hangs thick over the water, which now runs low and sultry. We park, heave the canoe over our heads onto the pavement, then tote it down to the bank, where dozens of canoes are lined up like orderly, beached fish. By 7:30 the temperature reaches the nineties, and by 8:00 the crowd has swelled to hundreds. Everyone mills about in baseball caps and fishing hats, slathering on sunscreen and guzzling water. Friends of the Mississippi River, the nonprofit that organized this celebration, herds us into pods of twenty-five canoes and lends each pod a well-tanned, husky-voiced leader. Ours is Kathy, sporting a purple life vest and a walkie-talkie on her hip. With Kathy in charge, our pod grows rowdy. We descend on the beach wielding paddles, wearing PFDs, and sweating profusely.

Jorge crawls in and I shove off, feet dragging in the cool water. A slight chill rises from the surface. Overhead, the sun is merciless. Our flotilla—a collection of city dwellers who are, for the most part, strangers to one another—begins unified and jovial but then spreads thin across the river's width. We dip and swing, noting the familiar landscape from this fresh, buoyant perspective. There's the concert hall, the hospital, the Witch's Hat tower! So this is what the Franklin Avenue Bridge looks like from below! The water shimmers with heat. Today the Mississippi is tamed, muddy, and sluggish, polluted through and through by agriculture, industry, automobiles, and the daily trash of residents. We pass an egret, a nude bather, a sunken tire, a Mexican family fishing. Small-mouth bass flap and splash in our vision's periphery. Jorge identifies rocky eddies where he'll return to hunt for mud puppies, and I delight in the swallows swooping toward pockmarks in the sandstone cliffs. We have a lovely morning, bantering with our canoe neighbors, basking in the heat, receiving periodic lectures on river history (what is now St. Anthony Falls in Minneapolis has retreated upstream from St. Paul over the past 10,000 years) and ecology (the bald eagle's return, the damage of urban runoff), and all the while I have this nagging suspicion that none of us knows the river at all—not proficient Kathy, slickly turning in her kayak, not the U of M specialists nor Park Service volunteers, not Jorge who spends his every free warm-weather moment measuring water quality and the health of aquatic life. This morning spent slipping over the Mississippi's surface is as yet seeing through a glass darkly. When, O God, will we see eye to eye?

For fourteen years now, I've drunk the Mississippi, strained and distilled in our treatment plants. I am more river than anything else. It's a wonder I don't burst in the spring and shrivel in late July. Sometimes when I meditate, I try to move into those muddy, sloshing cells and inhabit the world as they do, all gravity and liquid determination. Paddling on the river's surface, I am less certain than ever of my identity, rinsed as it is with others' lives and the muscled flow of river. When we come to the great lock and dam at Ford Parkway, our caravan of canoes huddles to the right, guided by red buoys, avoiding the sudden, swift current at the edge of the falls. A hundred canoes at a time, we are corralled into the lock's metal hull, the huge doors swinging shut. Overhead, black clouds loom from the west. The water level slinks down the slippery walls until we're lost in this cavernous, echoing, shadowed space. It is an artificial but practical transition from one altitude to the next—such a human construction, so like identity in that we need the limited, controlled image of self to proceed, and all the while who we are roars alongside, over the falls. Once the lower doors open, our canoes scoot out into seething white water. We speed round the bend, then beach at Hidden Falls, where volunteers await us with sandwiches and sodas. In the celebratory aftermath, the day's heat finally shoots lightning; crowds dash to the park pavilion holding life jackets over their heads. Suddenly water is everywhere—angling to earth in sheets, streaming along park paths, sullenly and steadily flowing southward with the Mississippi, in and through our bodies, and it seems I could forget myself in a flash, washed away in this conflux.

By the time Jorge and I retrieve the car, load up the canoe, and hit the road, the storm has swept eastward and steam rises in the trees over the gorge. We turn across the Mississippi at the Ford Parkway, slowing midway to admire where we've been: that turbid surface, seemingly unchanged for our having touched it. I suppose it's impossible to maintain a self-image that includes all of identity's permutations. I can't know how a stranger ingests my words; I can't fathom what part of me (if any) Mr. Pasierb encompasses, nor, for that matter, Leona, in her current unfettered form. Were I to attempt a constant awareness of self spread across community, landscape, and time, I'd fly apart at the seams. What difference does it make, then, to consider identity a flaccid construct? With the river again contained below me, I wonder whether it isn't more natural to glimpse self's vastness only rarely, forgetting our smallness as the Mississippi forgets its retaining walls and submerged wing dams during each decade's rough-and-tumble flood season. When identity swells, spills over and sinks in, we recollect our wider being. Then we return to life with a softening memory of unity, able to carry on.

An Absence

THE FLABBY KID ACROSS THE STREET learned to drive last winter; he spent a few weeks screeching around the corner in his mother's hulking Suburban. Then he disappeared again into the dark cavity of his house. Last month, he stood in the front doorway screaming at his sister; she slammed her car door and peeled away. Since then he has not left the house. It's possible I've missed seeing him head to the corner store or on a late night stroll around the block. It's possible he's employed at home, or suffering from a chronic disease, or avidly building toy trains. But I doubt it. I feel his presence like a black hole, a dense, swirling force drawing all energy and attention inward. A shade remains drawn across his bedroom window. The cessation of his harassment frightens me more than his rude words ever did. At least when he called me names he was engaged with the world, facing the light of day, expressing his miscreant opinion. Now, I imagine, he boils with hatred and boredom and terrific waste. The neighborhood quiet is eerie, like the hush before a bomb explodes. This, it occurs to me, is the evil side of silence: lidded anger, self imploded upon self, the unyielding magnetic pull of a living absence.

Hail

*T*WO JUNIOR HIGH GIRLS sit at my dining room table writing circus stories, tales of high-wire acts, wailing children, and clown careers gone awry. One writes in green magic marker; I wonder how she can abide the sweet lime smell. Their handwriting is wide and loopy, their spelling atrocious. I teach them about revision, a difficult notion for concrete thinkers, by having them exchange stories and choose a section to "stretch." They draw arrows into each other's texts and expand a moment, one by flashing back to the circus performer's bleak childhood, the other by elaborating on the trapeze artist's sweaty palms and thumping heart. The girls are bent over their spiral notebooks as though they have passed through the page into the spotlight of the dusty big top. Outside the house the sky turns dark, then threatening, then tornado green. The recessed light above the table shines on our imaginative cartwheels, separating this circle from the rest of the turbulent, rainy city. Then it's hailing milky white ice the size of marbles—no, the size of ping-pong balls—and the three of us look up from our pages toward the window pocking with hail, the hail splashing in Evelyn's gutters, hail knocking small branches off the evergreen, thudding on the roof, slicing through the rhubarb leaves, polka-dotting the grass. One girl says, "I've never seen it this big." The other: "Where does it come from? It's so warm out." We watch round ice land in the street and bounce (a plague? a comedy?); we watch it dent the hood of a parked car. The storm thrashes the city then slows, grows small. Before turning back to our stretched moments around the bright oak table, the three of us look at one another, our eyes wide as hail.

Baptism

No PRAYER IS AS BUOYANT as an afternoon swim. Down at the bottom, where carp maneuver among the mud and reeds, where their bulging eyes discern one shadow from the next, the northern Minnesota lake (no swimming police here!) remembers forty-below wind chills—weather that made it solid and formidable. All summer long, even while deer flies buzz the water's surface and glittering dragonflies dip and rise, even after the heat index kicks in and children have splashed and Marco-Poloed and dolphin-dived because it is the only sane thing to do under such unbearable sun, even then, the water remembers winter and bites when I first dangle my toes. For a moment I cling to the dock.

I leap, suddenly up to my waist in the previous season, a chill licking the hollow of my spine, creeping up my neck and setting my arm hairs on edge. Ruthless, I dive in. I swim through the initial shock. The only way to warmth is through this bitter blast to the bones, breast stroke in double time the way Olympic racers swim, beginning one breath even before the last is finished. I swim madly until I break through the numbness. I'm halfway across the lake by the time I slow down and check in with my toes—yes, I can feel them, yes, my heart pounds. Fresh water is on my lips, tasting slightly green and sweet like rain on a honeysuckle blossom.

And then, eyes closed, I swim the breast stroke the way a yogi might, noticing the stretch as arms extend, breathing into the pull, tucking my legs under, imagining the cold-blooded, lean body of a frog, then thrusting forward with the rush of surface water streaming past. My right arm and leg are stronger than my left, sending me into perpetual circles. The shore is far away, other swimmers are far away, and the only creature I run into is a fish, scales brushing skin like a chance touch on a city street. We're both in our element. I match the rhythm of my breathing to the stroke—arms, legs, and lungs contract; arms, legs, and lungs release. The air that enters me also propels me. I convert air to movement through water. All I hear is the inrush and outrush of breath, the fabulous workings of human anatomy. Every cell floats and every muscle pushes me forward.

I roll onto my back. The sun is out, warming my face and the water's surface. Behind my eyelids I see the stained glass colors of skin on a clear day—lemon yellow, burnt orange, burgundy speckled, and when I open my eyes there are sunspots, blinding blotches that pulse the way stars do. Water touches me and lifts me up; the air enters and lifts me up; I am buoyed, held, surrounded, loved. I float on the cusp of the elements, a solid form hovering between liquid and gas. Now I reside in all four dimensions and am aware of it, the length of me pulled taut along the water's surface, the depth of me half sunk but still afloat, the width of me drinking in sunlight, and time entering and exiting my lungs. So this is balance. I might be asleep, my mind is so quiet.

When the sun slides behind a cloud, I can open my eyes and idly watch the blue that masks endless space. The atmosphere is a protective bubble. Wind and clouds flit from west to east following invisible channels, but then an osprey appears, outlining one rising current with her curved wing. This is as much as I'll ever see of the wind—a bird midair, seemingly still; the poplar leaves shimmering along the shore; a ripple sweeping over the lake, then dissolving. It dries my face. I float on a reflection of sky until suddenly I'm chilled and must move again, a water bird recklessly flapping as she tries to take off. The back stroke, arms cartwheel, legs kick. I actually move in a straight line, keeping my nose toward the one lone pine pointing above the rest.

There's no warming up now, despite my frenzy. As I near the shore, I remember what the lake remembers—the tremendous depth of things. Memory filters down and resides in layers of silt along the bottom, stirring only when I sink my feet into its weedy mush. Water was my first element, even before breath. I can't recall my mother's resounding heartbeat, but I can now hear my own, pulsing along the walls of my body; yet it is not mine at all but the pulse of the earth, this lake her womb. I am born over again, a thousand reincarnations in one lifetime. If prayer is anything, it is remembering this. I climb out onto shore like an amphibian, wincing at the solidity of this new home.

The Welcome

What is a house but a bigger skin,
and a neighborhood map
but the world's skin ever expanding?
—*Annie Dillard*

Ode to Earthworms

It's been four years since I invited you to my compost, offering kitchen scraps, leaves, and grass clippings as my welcome, and finally you appear, elongating your thick body around grapefruit rinds and spent bulbs. From what soily underworld do you arise? I don't understand your sudden emergence, nor how the sun can contract you to a stubby finger. I refuse to touch your pale translucence. Eater of coffee grinds, you disgust me; dung burrower, you fill me with awe! Exposed, you thrash your pink tail (head?) in frustration. I ought not lay eyes on you. Swiftly, I shovel out soil black with your castings and turn it under my tomato plants. I don't understand how offal feeds the earth or why the shovel blade, splitting your body, only multiplies life. How like a god you are! My own refuse is far less fecund. In it, I again bury you, you who languish in the light.

On Learning to
Like Olives at Age 33

$\mathcal{M}$Y COUSIN ALICE used to slip one on each fingertip, asking her mother to cap her thumbs, then cockily flashing ten black-nobbed indices at me while I made faces back. She popped each olive into her mouth, her lips forming the perfect olive-O.

It looked like fun, but I felt no envy because I knew the black tar taste, like the salty scum mustaches we acquired swimming in the Hudson River before it was cleaned up. Back then, olives were easy enough to avoid. My mother disliked them as much as I did and never cooked with them, although my father occasionally treated himself to a small container of specialty olives that he kept in the fridge. Outside of home I discreetly pushed them off the pizza, handed the condiments over, and ignored Greek salads on restaurant menus. After I passed that mysterious marker into adulthood (when we can no longer be demonstrative about our taste dislikes), I learned to stomach olives in potluck salads and in those Minnesotan vegetable hot dishes as a discipline of politeness. Olives, even the imported ones, were a bitter, black putridity or slimy green acid that made dinner most unpleasant.

But then Jorge, who is Puerto Rican, bought red snapper one evening, scoured the skin with garlic, stuffed the fish with capers and Spanish olives as his grandmother taught him, and pan-fried them while I stood in the garlic fumes, worrying that I might not survive the meal. We sat down at table around a platter of two golden fish fat with olives, each with a single, cooked eye cocked at the ceiling. My first bite bewildered me. The second tingled my palate. The olives were multidimensional, a slight sour followed with a potent, fruity zing. Salty olive green had sunk through the loose white fish flesh, balancing mild with pungent, creature of the ocean with fruit of the land, and I couldn't scrape enough off the fragile rack of bones to satisfy my craving for this paradox.

After Jorge's meal came the olives-on-a-stick at the Minnesota State Fair—four plump olives packed with garlic, sundried tomatoes, pimentos, onions, each pregnant with flavor. Rolling one on my tongue, I drank its acrid sweat before the initial, stunning bite. On one weeklong silent retreat, we were served a tapenade to dollop on our soup. I watched as the leftovers got scraped into a jar and refrigerated. For days afterward, pureed kalamata olives appeared in my prayers. I'd focus on my breathing and almost pass into that pure space of internal silence when I'd see bruised gold swirled among lentils or spread on toast, and be overtaken with a craving to sneak a spoonful of purple pleasure right from the jar. Perhaps it was gluttony, for me not an unfamiliar sin. Or perhaps the soul's movement suddenly shifted, taking my taste buds' conversion as a cue for what is always possible: the sudden widening of our loves.

Block Party

DRIVING ACROSS TOWN after teaching tonight took twice the usual time. The city is barricaded; police lines block off most residential north-south avenues, making it look like we're under siege. There are plenty of causes for anxiety (crime, terrorism, war), but tonight my gravest worry is whether my tabouli salad will be too garlicky for the neighbors. It's National Night Out, an event devised by a nonprofit organization and promoted by police and crime prevention groups to introduce neighbors to one another. Really it's a city-initiated block party. If our block's organizer can muster up enough signatures, we get the street cordoned off and the police will send door prizes (Twins tickets or coupons for Valley Fair amusement park) to lure the residents out of their homes. The intent is to build connections. If we're familiar with our neighbors, we'll watch out for one another and the block becomes a safer place. From the looks of Minneapolis tonight, National Night Out is working.

After driving down the alley, parking, and retrieving my perhaps too healthy salad from the refrigerator, I walk up the street toward people clustered around a smoking kettle grill. The kids, ecstatic, bike down the center of the street. The little ones draw on the pavement with thick fingers of chalk. Adults stand together clutching pop cans or sit on folding chairs that they've had the foresight to bring from home. I say quick hellos—to Evelyn, who is wearing an ironed floral T-shirt; to Emmett and Judy, to the red-headed twins, and to Janelle, our block coordinator, who reminds me to make a name tag. Her eldest daughter, Latasha, has a black kitten on a leash who is suddenly curious about my toes. Latasha tells me how Midnight appeared in their bushes and how Latasha begged her mother to let her keep him. When I first moved onto the block, Latasha was a scrawny kid in pigtails. Four years later she looks me in the eye, her hair elegant down her back.

I place my bowl alongside the hamburger buns, Rice Krispy bars, and marshmallow fruit salad. Amy, who has a Guatemalan daughter she is raising bilingually, has brought fried plantains, and this makes my day. Evelyn has brought a deli vegetable plate. Bags of chips abound, and because I never buy them for myself, I gorge shamelessly. Duey, who has the best flower garden on the block, is flipping burgers and rolling brats. The twins' grandmother arrives with their unique concoction—two cookie sheets of cold vegetable pizzas. When I ask Chrissy about the recipe, she says, "You know that stuff you buy in the tube? That's the crust, and then you pour on spaghetti sauce and put on broccoli and mushrooms and cheese on the top. It's really good." I reply that I'm sure she's right, but I'm unconvinced. I load up a burger, replenish my chips, and find a spare cooler to sit on.

Gary, the one other resident on the block who is openly gay (or is it just me who recognizes the body language, the earring, and the meaning of our huddled camaraderie?) fills me in on his latest painting project. "I was down in Vegas this last April," he says, "and the lights just went right to my head. So I started working abstract for the first time." We banter around the idea of a joint reading/art show at the local café. Much to my surprise, he asks about my work, which my other neighbors find intimidating and therefore shun. Gary is interested in my life in a detached, neighborly way, and I feel a sudden rush of affection.

I check in with Emmett, who is devoting his retirement (after a post office career) to helping people fill out forms at the welfare office. "A lot of them can't read English," he tells me. "You know, they come from all over the world. Sometimes they tell me their stories." I imagine Emmett's grandfatherly posture and shy demeanor in that otherwise inhospitable place. Whenever I see him out in the yard, I gravitate his way just to look into his gentle, alert eyes. He invariably says, "Oh! Hi, there," as though he's surprised by my attention. His checked shirts with worn cuffs and belted-up polyester slacks comfort me, somehow.

Chrissy interrupts us. "Elizabethee!" she exclaims, hop-scotching over.

"Elizabethee?!" I repeat, mocking horror at her familiarity. She ignores me.

"Will you pay me and Abigail to pick the dandelions from your yard? Our dad got a dandelion picker." My dandelion situation must be offensive indeed if the neighbor kids offer to eradicate them. Earlier in the day I'd seen the two girls trying out the pogo stick contraption near my driveway. Neither one was strong enough to press the pointed metal jaws through the sod, and so the yellow heads popped off at the stems.

"I don't think so," I say. "You need to get the roots up, too." Chrissy flips her ponytail, unconcerned, and heads for the brownies.

Most of the picnic is spent in small talk—the theft from April and Erik's garage, whether the new light rail line will change the bus schedule, and how the city ticketed Evelyn for growing grass between the concrete tracks leading to her garage. "It's been that way for thirty-five years!" she exclaims with annoyance. "Why is it suddenly a problem now?" Some topics are never broached (where, for instance, are our neighbors from the flat-faced house?), while others are touched upon lightly—elderly Rose's death and the estate sale her family held, where I bought a crate of mason jars; the upcoming election; how Ernest Stringer across the street passed out drunk on his steps for the third time and April called 911. Flashing emergency lights on our block make any private occasion public. The block party would feel old-fashioned were it not for this odd assortment of people— the elderly contingent in lawn chairs, Duey with his long features and thick Native braid, Janelle bustling around the food table, the passel of kids, mostly from multiracial families. I watch the burly guy with tattoos on both shoulders smoke a cigarette; I watch his girlfriend, who wears tight jeans and a top that's not much more than a bandanna tied at her neck and waist. Her hips sway extravagantly; the kids look at her with reverence and fear. There is no other circumstance that would bring such divergent individuals together and force us into conversation. So what if we talk mostly about the weather?

When I approach withdrawn Duey to thank him for the barbecue and compliment his garden (a profusion of native plants— butterfly bush, black-eyed susans, phlox, milkweed), he becomes suddenly animated and offers me a tour. We cross the empty street to his home, banked in pinks and reds and purple. He'll be getting rid of some coneflowers in the fall; would I like a few? Already plants get passed up and down the block. I have April's blackberry and raspberry bushes, Evelyn has some of my bleeding heart, I've sent rhubarb up to Janelle, and Emmett and I swap currant bushes, garlic chives, bee balm, and coreopsis. I'd love to have Duey's coneflowers, which bend their prickly purple noses toward the sun. Even more, I am grateful for his enthusiasm, his sudden engagement, and the connection that's seeded between us now—our passion for growing things. Surely the block is a bit safer for all this cross-pollination.

Back in Janelle's yard, Evelyn is taking snapshots, the twins are playing with Midnight, and the burly guy has got his girl-friend in his lap. Yellow jackets make stabs at the plastic-wrapped food; there is still plenty. Janelle's husband rigged up their stereo on the porch and is playing James Brown; he's also turned on the Christmas lights. There's something awkward and embarrassing about this gathering, a sensation not unlike a blind date except that we already live side by side and know which couples scream at each other and which kids need new shoes. Perhaps it's this odd intimacy among relative strangers that makes us abashed in one another's company. I know the burly guy's retaining wall is falling down, but I don't know his name. Eventually I will, and perhaps he'll keep an extra eye on my house when he walks past with his chocolate lab each morning. Tonight police barricades section off the street, making way for hotdogs and small talk and reckless biking; tomorrow, the city will be overwhelmingly large again, a grid of homes and automobiles and crime. Perhaps the block party makes us shy because it's an investment in a fragile, invisible, nameless bond. Perhaps it is holy work—the only security that's ever proven trustworthy; the slow, mundane cultivation of community.

Beggars to God

I'M WEEDING IN THE BACKYARD, my knees in the dirt, my face in the acidic aura of tomato plants, when suddenly a Hmong woman is standing on my lawn not three feet away. I rear up in surprise, bumping against a tomato cage. I have left white Minnesota, where the boundaries around personal space are strung up like an invisible dog fence (even dear Evelyn feels strangely guilty entering my yard to pick produce while I'm out of town), for the mountains of Laos, where an open piece of land is simply land, unowned, unmarked, and an old woman can step forward fearlessly. She's two-thirds my height, so wrinkled her eyes have retreated into her face, her plain blouse loose against a shapeless chest. Except for the gray scalp between her thin strands of hair and her dusty, pink palm, her skin is a deep brown. She approaches me with her left hand forward, jiggling four or five pennies. Her right arm clutches a loaf of Wonder Bread against her waist. The way her shoulders roll forward makes her seem tired, almost beyond caring. She's muttering in her native tongue (or is

it an old lady's language?) but still, I can understand the plead-
ing tone. Her eyes are wide with need.

I yank a few carrots from the ground, pick a ripe tomato, and
motion that I'll be back in a minute. Inside the cool kitchen, I
rinse the vegetables, empty a drained can of tuna into an old yo-
gurt container, gather some peanuts, cookies, and plastic uten-
sils, and put them all into a paper bag. I am my mother packing
lunch on a school day, the brown bag filling with both food and
prayer—that the world not be too cruel, that bread and vegetables be understood as love, that deep hungers might be satisfied
as well as bodily ones. Except I am not packing lunch for a child,
but for a woman slightly stooped, a woman whose people sided
with democracy on the losing side of a war and then were chased
from their mountains across the ocean to their ally, who could
but would not feed them. What insanity, that the grandmothers
of suffering must beg to eat! I fold the paper bag closed over my
longing (might the world be otherwise?) and push the screen
door open into sunshine.

She is standing where I left her, the copper pennies still
glinting in her palm. I hand her the lunch sack and say, "Here
you go; I hope this helps," not so much for the words' meaning
(she doesn't understand) as to cover with sound how awkward I
feel feeding her. She slips the pennies into her pocket, looks me
in the eye, and mutters. In no way does she seem obliged or
grateful. Except that she grabs the sack from me, shuffles back
to the alley, and immediately sits on the low cement retaining
wall to begin eating, desperately hungry, biting into the tomato,
picking up pieces of tuna with her fingers and shoving them into
her mouth, ravenous to the point where I can accept her ingrat-
itude because nothing, nothing, will satisfy this need, least of all
the humble lunch I've provided. Here is tragedy grown old. Here
is grief beyond caring, the sins of the world having consumed a
tired woman's body and irony having fed her, insufficiently. She

bends over her meal, protective although no one is around. She does not look up.

To give her some privacy I kneel back into the garden's black soil. Crabgrass, clover, dandelions, and creeping charlie all gnaw on the roots of my tomato plants, and I try hard not to despair as I yank them out, day after day, an entire summer of effort. My prayers are insatiable. Weeds, like poverty, we will always have with us. I rip grass from the earth ruthlessly; I fling frustrated handfuls into a pail never big enough to carry all these troubles away.

Space for Company

IF MY HOUSE IS A BOOK, the bedroom is the chapter I dread writing. Readers are welcome in the more habitable rooms, in the office with its wicker rockers, the living room crowded with plants, the kitchen where sunlight blazes across a poetry-plastered refrigerator. In the bedroom, the unfinished platform bed I bought years ago remains pale and rough, the ceiling paint is strangely peeling in one corner, and I've never gotten around to stripping the dark, sticky varnish off my antique desk. The room is so crowded, I rarely have the energy to wind the vacuum around the furniture or wipe cobwebs from the ceiling. It's a small space, nine by ten, and the full-size bed means that I can't easily get to the windows. The drawn blinds lend the room a perpetual gloom. When guests arrive, I discreetly close the door.

The bedroom's dismissal of company doesn't make me proud. Here is a place inhabited only in sleep and in the quick nakedness before dressing. The unmade bed emanates loneliness. The lavender walls speak more to the previous owner's passion than my own. In its language of wood, fabric, paper, and filth, my room tells me plainly what I once paid a therapist good money to clarify—my life hasn't fully welcomed intimacy. Left to natural inclinations I retreat into bachelor-style disarray, hanging a Do Not Disturb sign from the doorknob.

Recently, however, I've had occasion to ponder the power of will and our capacity to bring about change. If there's space in my home where I resist company and I *will* it otherwise, perhaps it's best to begin by opening the door and flicking on the light switch. Take a look. Here is the intimate room of a woman single too long.

Is it resignation that scents the air, or unfulfilled longing? For ten years I dated casually, worrying whether my standards were too high ("I need someone with a big soul," I whined to my friends, unable to articulate what, exactly, a big soul might look like) or if my capacity for intimacy was somehow faulty. High school and college friends paired off with seeming ease. I was stranded in my thirties possessing limited flirtation skills, attending a church that more sensible individuals had forsaken, and balking at the singles scene both gay and straight. For want of a guilty party, I vacillated between blaming my generation of self-preoccupied, material-grubbing status seekers, my erotophobic parents (who, from my adolescence, had couched sexual intimacy in an ominous silence), and God. Mostly I blamed God. The universe itself seemed antagonistic, introducing me to person after person with needs I could not tolerate. This high-strung woman was on the rebound. That man—the one who engaged in a solo discussion about his ministry over dinner—was stuffed with ego. Surely fate had conspired against me. All the good people were taken.

Slowly, insidiously, I slipped into theological fatalism. Everything that happens, I rationalized, is supposed to happen. *I'm meant to be single* became an internal refrain that exaggerated itself, during my more grandiose moods, into *Perhaps I'm called to be celibate*. Quite possibly this relational wasteland was ordained by God. After all, pent-up sexual energy finds release in creative expression, which was undoubtedly my vocation. Celibacy has an appealing aura of holiness, at least in the abstract. If the mighty will of the world makes itself known de facto in the inevitable unfolding of circumstance, then at least my solitude served some purpose. Even if I would never understand it; even if I continued to despise it.

I had stumbled into the old joke: If you want to make God laugh, tell her your plans. You think you're going to school for a business degree and wind up in botany. You assumed you were straight until you encountered that first, ravishing same-sex lover. I'd imagined my life proceeding much as my parents' had (a solid and sustainable marriage coming early, easily) with bisexuality and its gender-neutral playing field the only variation. My parents met on a blind date in college, remained faithful through my father's obligations to the military, and sealed their commitment with seeming ease before age 28. My plans for a similar fortune grew suspect as I entered my fourth decade. A few more years of singleness convinced me that the universe had its own plans, steamrolling mine with the smooth passage of time. I beat the pillows in frustration.

Perhaps the will of God is like this. You kneel before your candle in prayer. You assume the omniscient Spirit hovers around you, hearing your pleas, responding, when suddenly you see how *seventeenth century* this notion is; you might as well believe the sun revolves around the earth. Suddenly God is the heavy pull of gravity, and, from your random point on this spinning globe, the heavens are neither up nor down.

The bedroom was barren and I shunned it. The dust on the dresser, the bed's raw wood, the closet jammed with only my clothes depressed me with their curse—I was not made for romance. Without my awareness, the sneaky tendrils of Christian tradition had wound a stranglehold around my thinking. Jesus was *meant* to be crucified; he was a sacrificial lamb offered up by God to cleanse us of sins rampant since Eve willfully yanked the apple. God must have intended Jesus to die because that's what happened, and Jesus knew it would happen. St. Augustine extrapolated this interpretation of the gospel texts and infused the church ever after with the conviction that God is in control here; our own untrustworthy wills ought to submit to the righteous flow of God's grand intent. If something is meant to happen, it will. Our own desires for the world to be otherwise are sinful and suspect.

Why, then, did loneliness stalk me? I tossed in the bedsheets, aching for sexual contact, a whispered secret, and to read the newspaper, fart, and fold the laundry (in other words, be at home) in company. Unlike the vast majority of the human population, I was unworthy of love. My high school classmates had implied as much by their inability to imagine me, their valedictorian, ever holding a boy's hand. Certainly my parents confirmed this with their unrelenting discomfort around matters romantic. Resigning myself to fate only deepened my despair. My will for a partner was immutable, and contrary. What began as a bout of loneliness became a crisis of faith.

With fierce determination, I followed my ache into the therapist's office. On the couch, I recounted my first date—I was a high school junior, going to the senior prom with a fellow artist—and how my mother chased me around the house waving the makeup brush, shouting, "You *will* wear blush!" I related the more sinister warnings my sister and I received about our family's fertile propensities, without any accompanying instruction in birth control. The therapist prodded, and I told her my insecurities around intimacy. Sure, my family loved me, but why would anyone else? I couldn't imagine taking my date's hand during a movie without first asking permission. In my therapist's eyes, this was unacceptable. Other people's will held sway over my own, so my therapist began a campaign to get me to be naughty in compensation. She intentionally used language so foul that my own vocabulary took a colorful turn. I got drunk; I forced my way through poorly written lesbian erotica; I bounced checks; I reneged on commitments. I made out with women I didn't care for, just to see what it felt like. For the first time in my life, I said no to what I knew to be right. The rebellion I was too good to engage in as a teenager seemed awkward in my thirties, pointless even, because I could see through it all to the lesson I needed to learn (test limits; take risks). But in the end the therapist was right—I had to experience lashing out; I had to try asserting my will in order to know that the world wouldn't collapse in response. To hell with God, I thought, launching into a streak of blind dates. If God, the universe, or whatever it is that causes circumstances to unfurl wasn't able or willing to pair me up, I'd make it happen by sheer exertion.

In the middle of one nasty fling, I went to church and heard the story of the prodigal son—the younger brother who made off with his half of the inheritance only to blow it and return home with his tail between his legs. Over a lifetime of churchgoing, I'd heard this story hundreds of times, always from the perspective of the older brother, the one who stayed with his father, because he was *me*, a thrifty, straight-A parent pleaser. I had imagined the younger brother sitting in the sty craving pig swill and thought, "What a loser!" Most sermonizers expound on the story's sin-and-repentance message; we stray from what's right, feel guilty, and return to a God more than willing to welcome us back to righteousness. The unspoken lesson, of course, was that the older brother was the real Christian. Stay close to home and do what's safe, the parable taught me. Avoid screwing up in the first place.

Never before had I heard the story from a place of defiance. I sat in the sanctuary pew, haunted by my date the previous evening (she skipped the foreplay and I didn't stop her), and the parable cartwheeled in my brain. The prodigal brother flew into his father's arms, got the fatted calf cooked up in his honor, and when I felt the familiar pang of jealousy—why should *he* get a party?—I suddenly wondered whether for us older siblings jealousy wasn't the story's point. The father stands by both sons, regardless of their chosen paths. In the end, it's the prodigal son's relationship with the father that is textured with sorrow, mercy, and a love that leaps across separation. His life is tempered. His shame transforms him. Beneath his fondness for women, drink, and riches, he discovers a stronger desire, one that enables him to walk into his fear and into a relationship more profound than any available to those of us who never take a risk.

I sat upright against the pew's hard back, astonished by the possibility that we're meant to be willful. Later I learned that the desert ammas and abbas, mothers and fathers who formed the first Christian monastic communities in Egypt, the Holy Land, and Asia Minor, were not, unlike the current crop of Christians, unsettled by sin. Rather, they saw sin as a crack into which God might squeeze to soften a person's soul. Sin was not errant; it was necessary. As Amma Theodora put it, "Just as the trees, if they have not stood before the winter's storms, cannot bear fruit, so it is with us; this present age is a storm and it is only through many trials and temptations that we can obtain an inheritance in the kingdom of heaven." By never stepping out into the world, by never experimenting, acting on our desires, or discovering our capacity for evil and good, we clutchers to security compromise our spirit. We cannot obtain the inheritance, which is an unbounded, prodigious capacity for love. The poet Czeslaw Milosz calls it "attachment to ethics at the expense of the sacred." Perhaps, I thought as I eyed the stiff congregation, we each need to take our money and run naked toward desire. It would bring us to ruin, and to a fortune greater than we can conceive.

The will of God, then, is like this: a no-man's-land between the old country and the new, tumbleweeds spinning in dust, a mirage on the horizon, and sudden disorientation. Now what's the direction we're heading? And why? At some point, stumbling forward blindly becomes easier than asking. There are none of the old signs—slashed lines in the road, stop, yield, and merge. Slowly you cease straining your neck. The thirst of the body takes over, pulling you across the landscape.

It's time to redecorate, to strip the bed, move the mattress into the dining room, carry out stacks of dusty books, empty the drawers of clothes, get rid of the overstuffed chair, and clean out the desk; it's time to sand down the window sills, the patch of peeling ceiling paint, the unfinished platform bed. I vacuum four years of cat hair from under the dresser. I push the windows wide and pry open a can of stain. When I swipe the soaked rag along the bed's grain, pine turns to wet teak; sworls and knots darken to a rich resonance.

I want my room to be a welcoming place, fostering intimacy and play, comfort and rest, but more than that I want my heart itself to be hospitable—to be light yet sturdy in upholding love. I'm not so simple as to believe we can rearrange our internal furniture (behavioral patterns, priorities, and preferences) simply by pushing the desk against a different wall and staining the bed a new color. Real change takes effort and time. Still, I can't help but hope the corresponding pieces of my heart will reconfigure themselves as I work. Or perhaps redecorating is a way of solidly manifesting in my external life what is tentative and new inside of me. I need physical reminders, lest I slip back into old ruts. Overhead, the ceiling fan draws in cold air. I'm on my knees, caressing every surface of my bed with a ripped T-shirt, calling forth from the wood what's been hidden there all along—its streaked and grainy warmth.

Every summer I offer a weeklong writing camp to the kids at church. It started when an eight-year-old burst into tears because she wasn't old enough to take a public class I was teaching. After that we made arrangements for Kayla and five other kids to spend afternoons with me, scratching poetry onto the sidewalk and telling ghost stories in the basement. Over the years, Kayla's figure and her prose have fleshed out. Instead of handing me bulletins with penciled poems after church, she asks me to critique her school speeches and attend readings for contests she's won. The full force of her transformation didn't strike me, however, until the fourth year of camp. Kayla strode into the house wearing bell-bottoms, commented snidely on every exercise, and refused to allow anyone's attention to stray from her teenage witticisms. The bright, fanciful girl had become an adolescent monster. During writing time, Kayla made lists of her friends' inside jokes, then worked herself into a giggling frenzy when I asked her to share. I wanted to strangle her. She was ruining the easy, focused spirit of the camp. When I complained to friends from church, they assured me that Kayla's rudeness was a compliment. She trusted me enough to test my limits.

In a way, I was in awe of Kayla. She was immersed in the full-fledged teenage rebellion I had skipped, scorning her mother, obsessing about boys, saying a broad no to everyone's expectations. I wanted to shake some sense into her but also cheer her on. If she could test the boundaries of willfulness now, her adult decisions would be based on desire rather than obligation or fear. By annoying me and despising her mother, Kayla was learning that she didn't have to earn love from the adults in her life. For the first time, I felt myself in the prodigal parent's shoes. No wonder the father turned over his savings so readily.

About that same time, I had lunch with Al, a fellow congregant who was also writing a book. Together we bemoaned the many distractions that pull us from our work. Just that morning, Al told me, he'd gotten a call from the church secretary. "She must have a limited list of who's home during weekdays," he said. "She wanted me to come in and help fold the newsletter." It's too easy when you are a member of a small urban parish to get sucked in to the million and one tasks that keep a congregation vital—driving members to the airport, delivering meals-on-wheels, attending committee meetings, making banners, marching in protests. . . all connective work that creates community. If you let it, church will consume your every moment.

"Now, I'm not opposed to doing office work," Al said firmly, pointing his fork at me, "but I've got to draw the line somewhere. I'm beginning to figure, if I ever want to say an enthusiastic yes to church, I first have to be able to say no." Immediately I thought of Kayla, and how much more confident she will be as an adult for having exerted her will as an adolescent. Then I thought of all the lukewarm yeses I've heard from Christians over my lifetime, agreeing to serve as building trustee year after year because the church would collapse if they quit, cleaning up after coffee hour because they *should*, disgruntled and exhausted but unable to be selfish enough to take a break. Moral propriety takes precedence over inner desire. When there is an external need, we Christians feel a righteous obligation to respond, even at the expense of our own well-being.

That's when I recognized another layer to the fallacy of sin. Christians believe we can't say no to God. By whatever means we've perceived God's will (through Scripture, through the needs of others, or even our own dreams), once we've discerned it we have to follow. Meanwhile, it's one of the great ironies of any dogmatic religion that the most solidly faithful are those who have, at some point, left. Without the option to doubt, to question, to sin, we miss the possibility of *choosing* to believe. Only intentional faith, born of free will, has real substance.

At the apex of my naughtiness, I knew myself to be straining against God. I determined not to be good if my notion of goodness stood in the way of intimacy. Without the option to say no to my singleness, my yes to partnership had been wishy-washy and resentful. In a bizarre twist, I suddenly understood that I was *meant* to say no to God. Or I needed to defy the remnant of that personal, controlling God who yielded influence in my relationships. Why was he still in my head? I had to learn the scope and power of my own will.

Chaos reigns. Deep cleaning, literal or figurative, entails conditions first getting worse. The bedroom project is a case in point. By Friday night I've painted a coat of stain on the platform bed, but the lamp and new bed stand are in the bathroom, the mattress leans against the dining room wall, the bedroom door, off its hinges, rests against the piano, the closet is floor-to-ceiling clothes, and stacks of books are scattered throughout the house like stalagmites, along with the boards and logs I use as bookshelves. I'm in a sneezing mania from the dust. When I unfold and make the living room futon for a night's rest, the entire house is disrupted. At 2:00 A.M., on my way to the bathroom, I trip over a log and whack my hip then my head against a misplaced chair. Rhia spends the night in the basement.

Ironic that, during my quest for relationship, I found myself increasingly surrounded by activists fighting for peace and working against the systemic racism that governs our foreign and domestic security policies. It shocked me to learn how dangerous it is to march against war, work for the Green Party, or stand vigil at the School of the Americas, even in a country that fiercely honors freedom. Anyone who presses for change faces some contemporary form of crucifixion. Friends working against U.S. sanctions in Iraq have FBI files inches thick. When crowds protest the lack of democratic process in our leaders' decisions to globalize the economy, the media slanders them by portraying only vandalism and passing over the police-perpetrated violence. I've come to admire people who believe their physical presence can affect even unwieldy institutions and who raise their voices despite severe personal consequences—and the occasional futility of their efforts. They are peaceable marchers, walking through fear toward a new form of justice.

In light of such radical dedication, the theology governing my quest for relationship gradually revealed itself to be faulty. Surely Jesus knew the political climate of his times. You don't go around the Roman Empire declaring that the very stone the builders rejected has become the cornerstone without risking your neck. So the man didn't need divine insight to foresee the consequences of his message. And the idea, not much evidenced in the Bible, that Jesus' death was intended to cleanse the rest of us of sins undercuts and thereby renders meaningless the thirty-three years he spent growing, preaching, tending the lepers, walking mile after mile, conversing with prostitutes, and eating with tax collectors. It was Jesus' life, and not his unjust death, that yields redemption and hope. If Jesus was *meant* to die, his story makes no sense.

When I take Jesus seriously as an ordinary man, it's obvious he put his life behind something *not* meant to happen—loving connections, harmonious, justice-seeking communities, wholeness of body and spirit. He worked for change, exerting his dogged will into social structures and intimate relationships. God, I suspect, was behind him all the way, rooting for Jesus to succeed against the worst odds. Or perhaps God was the very stuff of Jesus' determination. The sorrow felt at the crucifixion had divine origins, as does any grief at wrongdoing. I even have a hunch that

God hoped Jesus might dissuade his followers from forming the cult of Christianity. We might be less complacent then, more willing to live by the man's example than to worship him.

If God—if the fierce, creative force behind each breath—can ache for something that doesn't happen, the world is an untrustworthy place to go looking for divine will. In my lonely state, the idea that singleness might be a calling (simply because I hadn't yet met a good match) was finally exposed as an excuse not to try. I stepped outside of my boundaries around intimacy that had felt safe but were in fact constricting. My romantic frame of mind was solid. I was ready to pursue or be pursued; I trusted my sanity and my sexual well-being. The lonely, resounding ache in my gut was a nudge. God was in my longing for love, I concluded, motivating these changes in me. Our desires for connection have holy roots.

And still I had no prospects.

Perhaps God's will is like this: a house built on cement pilings, the basement supporting the walls that hold up the roof. Rooms are measured and raised. When you buy a house you take on a construct within which you live, and with a few exceptions (put in a skylight here, an extension there) you allow the house to frame your waking, lovemaking, and eating. When the house slips subtly around your shoulders like an old blanket, it is home. The will of God is sleepwalking through your beloved house. You know the way. You know where the stairs are and when to duck your head.

Out of deference to my body's need for touch, I took regular massages from Bridget, mother of one of my young writers. One afternoon, Bridget flipped back the blanket and began to work on my legs. I lay prone, naked, half asleep. She kneaded my feet, working on pressure points that probed all sorts of recesses I couldn't identify; she pushed on muscles up and down the length of my legs. Then she held my right foot in one hand and my right knee in the other, and began a smooth, unpredictable movement, raising and lowering my leg, drawing figure eights in the air, bending the knee then straightening it as though stirring soup with my foot. I was so relaxed and helpless in Bridget's hands, I felt like a marionette. Bridget could have done whatever she wanted with my leg, with my whole body, and I'd be unable to defend myself. Suddenly I panicked. I was too vulnerable. On the outside I was relaxed, but inside I was fighting. Bridget gently moved my left leg through the air in odd twists until it no longer felt like my body at all, but rather some appendaged form where I'd ended up by mistake. My stomach heaved with resistance.

Later Bridget told me that this technique—unwinding—is taken from cranial sacral work. "You're in the lead," she said. "I'm listening to your limbs' natural rhythms and following where they want to go. The theory is that your limbs trace a path backward through the tension to their original, aligned relationship with the body." On another day, she did the same with my head, cupping it in her hands and tracking its erratic motion through the air. If what she says is true, then neither one of us is in control. The body has its own life, separate from my awareness. Over time, will I recognize this strange unwinding, my body's journey back toward original placement? Underneath my rebel self, who despises helplessness, is this fine-tuned alignment, what the Sufis call True Self, with its irrecusable will.

"Christ has no body now on earth but yours, no hands but yours, no feet but yours," wrote Teresa of Avila, the sixteenth-century saint. At its foundation, Christianity bespeaks an incarnational deity, the sacred dwelling within us. The notion is so incomprehensible that it gets lost in the progressive sweep of time. Had Teresa added, "Christ has no will but yours," she might have saved me some trouble.

Yet it's not so simple. True desire lies buried under layers of falsehood; the prodigal son fornicated first. If we trust each person to discern God's will, we wind up with abortion clinic bombers and terrorists crashing into high-rises. Who is to say when we've struck the lodestone of God's will within our own? Where is a measuring stick for divinity? And yet I have within me, as do most people, a growing sense of what is just and what's not, what uplifts humanity and what does not, what brings about individual wholeness and communal well-being. Rather subjectively, I call these *sacred,* and steer my life accordingly. The secret of the Sufis, the paradox goes, is that Sufism has no secret at all; our innermost consciousness remains secret only while unknown. But it's always there. The third step of twelve-step programs turns our will and lives over to the care of our Higher Power, which, amazingly, resides within. When Martin Luther King Jr. declared our moral responsibility to disobey unjust laws, he was counting on this same inner compass. Surely it exists, regardless of tradition or culture, buried under layers of deception and misunderstanding. All we can do is launch forward, put our passion behind whatever we will, and live, at the very least, lustily.

Then last spring, a woman I'd run into when speaking in Berkeley, California, insisted I meet a Minneapolis friend of hers because of our common interest in community building. It was another of those far-fetched blind dates I was growing accustomed to but kept pursuing, as T. S. Eliot wrote, "without hope / hope would be hope for the wrong thing." Emily and I drank tea together at an outdoor café along a busy Minneapolis street while a thundercloud lumbered across the skyline. If it was love at first sight, neither of us recognized it. Conversation touched on the challenges of communal living and on our mothers, both of whom had recently become queer rights activists in the United

Methodist Church. Emily herself had left the pew-bound, pulpit-driven church for the silence of the Quaker meeting. When a few splashes of rain hit the table, Emily made distracted finger paintings in the dust and I offered to drive her home.

Love seems arbitrary, haphazard, hardly written in the stars. "Did you feel *that spark?*" friends asked, as they did after all my dates. I was intrigued with Emily, but skeptical. She was a good deal younger than I and idealistic in an untested way. What is a spark, and how does it feel? Emily had worn her hair in pigtails, and her dark eyes were defensive and challenging. She held her chin at a confident, down-turned angle. Her movements, from the coffee counter to our sidewalk table and then later, sliding fingers through the table's raindrops, were a dancer's, smooth and sure. Beyond our shared interests, there was no immediate connection. But for the first time in years I felt hope.

Why was I stunned, then, when one well-meaning friend, on hearing about my first successful date, said, "See? I knew you just needed to put it out there." I had heard the New Age logic behind her comment before; if you open yourself to something you desire—if you "put it out there," sending this hope into the world through prayer, telling friends, and intentionally shaping your life—then the universe will respond in kind. So I want romance; I slave away in therapy, I have friends set me up with every single man and woman they know, I pray constantly. When I meet someone with potential, I could say that it worked. I could say that we are capable of changing our circumstances by following our inner longings toward satisfaction.

But I'm not thus inclined. For a decade I was single and lonely, and the fact that my life might be otherwise now feels more like luck than a deserved end. The world has never been a place where individuals have power over circumstance. Too many times, riding our will, however impassioned, gets us nowhere. The odds against us are stacked high—not by God but by our market-driven economy, by the historical weight of prejudice, by the unpleasant reality that what most feeds our souls is also radically countercultural. In my own paltry example, the likelihood of finding anyone who meets my high relationship standards (I want a careful listener, someone who values simplicity, a person of integrity and steady commitment) is slim. I remain skeptical that humanity's capacity to will something into being, even with hard work, comes with any guarantee. It makes me cringe when people sugar-coat privilege with magical if-then thinking—if I put it out there, work hard, listen for the spirit's movement, then I'll get what I want. Ten years of singleness convinces me that even God-given desires may not be fulfilled in this lifetime.

So the will of God may be like this: a blank face, an unresponsive world. What should you do with your life? *Silence.* Are you always meant to be single? *Silence.* Does God care whether your body heals? *Silence.* Eventually God's seeming indifference makes you crazy for meaning or direction. At last you turn to the only refuge, the one place of reliable desire—your own will, motivated by loneliness and stubborn hope. You defy God; you find your own answers. Only in the aftermath (as you settle into a vocation, into bed with a lover, into your own well-being) do you recognize a relief greater than your own—a holy spirit sighing, *at last.*

Monday morning, after a weekend of staining and polyurethaning, painting, scrubbing, and mopping—after hauling the overstuffed chair to Goodwill, dragging the mattress back in, moving the bed, and rehanging the door—strangely, I wake up facing west. It takes me a minute to remember, *This is my house, my room, my body.* The closed blinds are luminous. From under the covers I soak in the new arrangement, windows to my right and across the room, night table beside me, desk in the corner. Around the bed's periphery there is space to walk, to tuck in sheets and unfurl blankets. The wall behind my head is empty, the ceiling freshly white. The air smells of wood stain and orange cleaner. Rhia, undaunted by the bed's new orientation, has again found her spot curled against my hip. I consider the window, and which evening light–loving plant I might hang there. The room is still mine; I still wake within its walls, alone. But soon I will rise; I will mark the new day by fluffing the pillows, tightening the sheets, and smoothing my mother's fine-stitched quilt across the broad bed. The door I will leave wide.

Thus the tenet I'm willing to stake my faith on is this: our core desires are worth striving for despite the odds because even if we never attain them, the changes that occur in us during the process are perhaps the purpose. When I considered that mundane conversation with Emily and still chose to give her another try; when I asked her dancing and planted that first, clumsy permissionless kiss on her lips, what was extraordinary was not the wave of affection, begun on a calm sea and swelling, its momentum toppling forward, but the transformation I recognized within me—a sudden, bold recognition of my worthiness for love. Nothing is certain about a young romance. The solid ground I'll stand on instead is this hospitality in my heart that effort and grace have made possible.

Tools

"**Y**OU DON'T HAVE TO BRING YOUR TOOLS," I told my dad over the phone. He was coming from New York for a weekend, and I had planned for the two of us to tackle the front porch, where a step was rotting and paint peeling from the floor and window sills. "We can always borrow some from my friends."

When I picked him up at the airport, a fifty-pound suitcase tumbled down the baggage claim. "I'll get that," he protested when I reached for the handle and could barely lift it.

Sure enough, when he unpacked, his clothes were tucked in a little plastic bag and the rest of the luggage was jammed with an electric sander, a battery-operated screwdriver, clamps, wood glue, sandpaper, a paint scraper, caulking gun, and other miscellaneous metal contraptions for which I didn't know the purpose. I had to laugh; did he mistrust my feminist friends' discernment among hardware? Did he think stores scarce here in the Minnesota backwater? What is it about a man and his tools? I showed him the porch, how the floorboards had buckled slightly, pushing back the paint, and how wood under the front step was spongy with rot. He brushed his hand along the flaking sills and said, "It's a good thing I brought my tools."

So we changed into work clothes (he in denim shirt and jeans with red suspenders) and got down to business. We moved furniture off the porch onto the lawn, dragged out the extension cord, revved up the sander, and began disturbing the summer afternoon with our dusty enterprise. I scraped and sanded the floor while my dad crouched on the steps to patch and seal the bad plank.

It wasn't long before Evelyn came out to rake her leafless lawn and cast curious eyes in our direction. "If you run out of things to do," she half joked, "I could always put you to work."

"Do you need help with something?" I asked, having grown savvy in the art of Scandinavian communication.

"Oh, it's just a screw I can't tighten. Nothing to worry about." Evelyn waved her hand dismissively.

My dad straightened from his work and beamed. "I'll get my screwdriver," he said.

He walked through Evelyn's false protests and tightened the screw in her fence. I watched, wondering how long Evelyn had been bothered by her troublesome screw and why my father, with his accompanying tools, could so suddenly become a neighborhood ambassador.

When the twins got off the bus from summer school, they ran up to sit in the rocker and chairs that were, strangely, on the lawn. "Who are you?" they demanded of my father, staring at his peppery beard.

"I'm the hired hand," he said.

"He's my dad," I explained.

They watched flakes of white paint chip off under his scraper, exposing the raw, weathered wood beneath, and insisted on helping. "Hold it this way," my father instructed, relinquishing his job into less efficient hands. Chrissy scraped while Abigail helped me hose down the screens. "Are we going to get paid for this?" Abigail asked. My father laughed, then waited for my response. I told her, as he might, that I'd pay them in Girl Scout cookies. The girls worked until their cousin got off the bus and wandered over.

"Here," Chrissy handed Erik the scraper. "You push with this sharp side." Soon enough, Erik was doing Chrissy's job and she was swinging from the porch railing. My dad asked her if she'd ever read Tom Sawyer. "I've seen the movie," she replied, missing his point. His mischievous eyes met mine over Chrissy's head, and he inquired whether the movie was any good.

I gave them all cookies and let Chrissy show Erik the checkerboard bathtub with red toenails before sending them home to do their schoolwork.

My dad and I swept, poured hardener into the floor's soft spots, and got out the primer. When he pulled two paint brushes from his suitcase, I knew that my father's preparedness was not a comment on my friends' tools nor on the availability of supplies in Minnesota so much as a manner of speaking, his tools really words in a worn, well-oiled language. The primer goes on, white over red, in sticky streaks; the wood filler dries under the front step. There are all sorts of things my father and I don't say, about my settling so far from home, about his desire for grandkids, about the odd, proud turn my life has taken from ordinary employment that allows me to be with him on a weekday. So he's brought tools to tell me what's most on his mind. He cares that my front step is firm. He cares that I'm bound to and loved by my neighbors. It matters that my windowsills last and that red paint seals the floorboards, one to the next, against moisture or insects or anything that might undermine my home's well-being. Together we heft the hammering weight of his language; we work on a house that holds us both for a weekend but is really the soul we, side by side, are learning to tend.

News

$\mathcal{A}$FTER FOUR YEARS of waving to Evelyn on Thursday evenings as we both haul bags of newspapers out to the recycling bins, I test the boundaries of our neighborly relationship by asking if she is willing to split a subscription to the *Minneapolis Star Tribune*.

Evelyn looks doubtful. "When do you read it?" she asks.

"Usually I don't pick it up till afternoon," I reply. "I can't bear to hear what's happening in the world before lunch."

Evelyn's face brightens at the sudden prospect of saving money. "I don't even get dressed until I read the news. That's my routine: Put on my robe, eat breakfast with the paper, and then I start my day."

I explain that I've been wanting a paper with better international news, but can't afford to subscribe to the *Christian Science Monitor* on top of the *Strib*, my source for local happenings. "Sharing a subscription would give me the best of both worlds,"

I tell her. On top of that, it'd be more environmentally sound, but this is an argument I don't mention.

"Yes," she concurs. "I have to get my other news from the *Weekly Standard*. Which," she adds pointedly, "isn't conservative enough for me."

For the sake of keeping the peace with Evelyn, I avoid certain topics of conversation, namely, religion and politics. Unfortunately, faith and civic duty are central to both our lives. Evelyn is active in her Norwegian Lutheran church; she keeps the Sabbath and reads Christian novels. On Election Day, Evelyn works the polls at the firehouse across Minnehaha Avenue, proudly signing each ballot as the neighborhood Republican. It's hard for us not to collide. Last primary, Evelyn leaned over her fence to complain about our choices. There were five candidates for mayor, all Democrats. Thus Evelyn's conundrum. "Who do you think I should vote for, Elizabeth?" she asked.

I hedged mightily. I remembered Evelyn's unabashed enthusiasm for the 2000 Republican National Convention. "Oh, Evelyn, you don't want to know."

"I do," she replied, stubbornly. "I asked. What, do you vote Green Party or something?" In Evelyn's vocabulary, Green Party is synonymous with the crazy couple down the street who complain when she sprays her lawn.

"Sometimes," I replied. "You know I'm more radical than you are. I just prefer to be private about my politics." *Good fences make good neighbors*, I was thinking. In Minnesota, where election lawn signs are more common than Christmas lights, my reticence is abnormal. Evelyn was justified in asking.

When I consider our fragile neighborly relationship, it seems risky to jointly subscribe to the liberal-bent local rag. Sharing resources smacks of anticonsumerism and communal living. But we're both single women living in single houses on limited incomes. Why shouldn't we be more generous with each other? Evelyn is sprightly but aging; throwing the paper out her backdoor onto my back steps will be a daily signal that she's well, especially through the winter when we hardly see each other. Neither of us will have to worry when we're away about the telltale sign of a stoop suddenly free of the morning newspaper. I write her a check, for which she's grateful. Afterward, I have an urge to do a victory dance—Evelyn and I have agreed on something!—and phone all my friends to tell them the news.

Messages

AFTER A WEEKEND AWAY, I return home to uncover penciled notes on slips of white paper tucked about the house in the oddest places. In the granola jar, one reads, "I love your eyes"; in the book I am reading, "I love your left armpit"; in my pencil basket, "I love laughing with you." Of course Emily has sneaked into my house and scattered her mischievous affection in my absence. At first it's her presence I feel, tucked between "merman" and "metalanguage" in the dictionary, but over time it's as though the house itself is speaking to me, or the universe, sending its grease-stained message in the peanut butter bucket. I used to look for God through the cracks of reality, expecting a pointed shaft of brilliance. But love is more substantial than that, and more mundane. Now God comes to me like bread, like dandelions, like a white slip falling from the blades of my ceiling fan when I first turn it on: "I love you! I love you! I love you!" it reads, with a sudden rush of air.

Praying in Place

VENUS IS RISING. From my living room window, I spot her hovering over a street lamp in the east. The corner grocery parking lot glows an unearthly orange and the city's haze blurs the black sky, but earth's sister planet, the goddess of beauty, is still visible. It is said she moves in radiant light. She pierces her way into my morning, putting the darkness of my house in perspective. I light a candle; I bend to my knees. My candle is small, swallowed up by looming shadows. But Venus is even smaller in the enormity of space. There's so much emptiness out there! No wonder cities huddle under clouds of artificial light. The sky is full of enough darkness that it could, without warning, enfold us in its terrifying oblivion.

I kneel before my window the same way my grandmother used to kneel before her bed—with great deliberation, as though her body knew humility and she simply yielded. I kneel in a small circle of candlelight, the house an indistinct expansive cavern at my back. Perhaps by taking time I can learn to live with all this emptiness. I want a quiet mind. I want to learn how to pray. The day, with its many complicated hours, waits across the street, behind rows of houses, across the Mississippi and below the horizon. My house waits too, its walls not yet solid with sunlight, its windows not yet alive with seeing. Even my furniture is formless in the shadows. Venus, who steals away the wits of the wise, is rising. I submit myself to gravity and the dangerous stillness of the present.

I know my grandmother knelt before bed because I peeked one night when I was little. My grandparents had matching twin beds, one two inches taller than the other to accommodate their respective heights, with real springs built into the frames. My grandfather died when I was seven, and after that, whenever we visited, my grandmother moved to the taller bed against the wall, giving me, her eldest grandchild, her own bed. Did she think Gramps' bed would frighten me? Or was it just harder for me to climb into? Grandma's bed felt the same as my bed at home, only I was aware that I was sleeping on air—I could hang my head over the edge of the mattress and peer between the metal curlicues.

Sent to bed long before the adults, I lay awake watching shadows from the streetlight and elm limbs play across the ceiling. The springs beneath me squeaked when I shifted. In the closet to my right, the mirror glinted above my grandmother's dressing table. I knew that tucked into its frame were photographs of us grandchildren and the crumpled drawings we'd sent her. My one-year-old hand print, pressed in clay, hung on the wall. From downstairs came the rattle and slam of backgammon dice and low murmur of family, minus my grandfather's husky voice.

A strange sensation overcame me before sleep, not only then but every night when I was young. I fell backward, turning heels over head through the blackness of space. There was no earth, no light, no point of reference; just a slow, effortless back dive through nothing. I was the hands of a great clock turning backward, only I was affixed to no face. There was nothing stationary with which to measure distance. It was both pleasurable and terrifying. I gripped the sheets in an attempt to stay attached to the bed. At Grandma's that night, I first spun backward through the recesses of the universe, then fell asleep.

Past midnight she tiptoed into the room, waking me. I lay still. She sat at the dressing table beside me to remove her nylons, and suddenly it occurred to me that she missed Gramps. Were I to roll over, Grandma's thoughts would first go to him. Gramps should be the one watching her step out of her wool skirt and straight-pin it to the hanger, not me. Her body was pale, lumpy at the waist. She gathered the flannel of her nightgown from the hem up until the neckline was at her thumbs, and then slipped it over her head. It fell lightly against her skin. Walking over to Gramps's bed, she eased her body down, slowly, to her knees.

I held my breath. I knew prayer to be something we recite in church, or said while holding hands around the dinner table, or shared with Mommy briefly before bed—a communal occurrence, spoken with and for others. That someone might offer up a personal prayer had never occurred to me. The picture books in Sunday school showed angelic children kneeling the way my grandmother knelt, at a bedside looking toward heaven, but I had never actually witnessed this kind of prayer. In reality it was more severe, more substantial. The night reeled around me. Through my slitted eyes, I sensed the privacy that my grandmother assumed in my sleeping presence. Death had left an extra, empty bed in the room. My grandmother knelt before it and before the window open to the dark sky. *Something magnificent is out there*, I thought; *something worthy and awesome*. I squeezed my eyes shut so as not to see.

꒰ꜛ꒱

They say if you die leaving unburned candles in your home, it's a
sign of a life not fully lived. I am burning my candles; I am learning to live each moment as though it's my last. Here in the depths
of the morning, I forgo kneeling to lie on my back. Through the
piano window high on the southern wall the stars are beginning
to fade. I try to recreate my childhood experience of flying backward. I want my prayer to be as complete and unrestrained as
that sensation. My imagination conjures up the gradual lowering
of the pillow and raising of my feet; I picture myself as a corpse
released from a starship, spinning in slow motion through the
great void. But my gut fails to believe it. I am exerting too much
effort. When I was a girl the sensation came unbidden, something that happened to me rather than something I made happen. It was a prebirth memory, connective, free.

At this point in my life, what's on the other side of death
comes not as memory but as premonition: *something mighty is
out there.* Venus is a point of light couched in vast darkness. Each
life is like Venus—a bundle of activity hurtling through a universe billions of light-years wide. Do I look for mightiness in the
specks of light, or in the space between? This planet I've got my
back against, with its oceans and continents and whorling, life-
giving atmosphere, is a miraculous anomaly. Perhaps there are a
great many such blips in the void, but, in proportion to the entirety, they are an "insignificant number," which my high school
chemistry teacher defined as the weight of cigarette ashes in the
armrests of an airplane compared with the weight of the whole.
Even if there are a thousand other life-supporting planets out
there, the breadth of this black universe is excessive in proportion. What is the purpose of so much nothingness? The quantity
stuns me.

Yet each morning I kneel before it. Whatever I suspect is out
there I want to welcome into my home and heart. Physicists call

space a creative vacuum; in order to support the explosion and implosion of energy that fuels life, a tremendous amount of nothingness is necessary. Without it there would be no planetary existence, no interplay between stars. Space is a reservoir empty enough to hold limitless possibility. Big bang; something comes from nothing. It's a creation story harder to believe than seven days and seven nights.

Even so, it's not all that different. *In the beginning God created the heavens and the earth. The earth was without form and void, and the darkness was upon the face of the deep; and the Spirit of God was moving over the face of the waters.* This morning and every morning, the earth is again without form. Darkness is upon my face. I am my grandmother, with her back to a child and her eyes on the heavens. With every prayer I step nearer to death.

I was seven when my grandfather had the heart attack that killed him. A heavy smoker in his earlier years, Gramps had a laryngectomy about the time I was born, and so his gruff voice emerged from the wrong place and scared me. Still, no one else read Brer Rabbit with such twang. I curled up on his lap and the strange, southern animals, full of chatter and misadventure, grew most vivid.

My family was moving from Los Angeles back to Tarrytown, New York, when we stopped in Utica to visit my grandparents. It was a homecoming—the errant Andrew family, not fit for West Coast living after all, returning to where we belonged. Gramps wasn't feeling well, but not bad enough to spoil the party. Until he stumbled down the stairs early Saturday afternoon with a pain in his chest.

I sat cross-legged on the living room carpet, a backgammon board opened expectantly in front of me. I was still young enough that adults were inexplicable, their movements a constant surprise. Only when I heard fear in Gramps' voice did it register that this was not right, that he was in danger—that our backgammon game would not happen after all. The house suddenly buzzed with activity. I sat, momentarily forgotten, the panic in the air absorbed into my frantic heartbeat and wide eyes. In a flurry of bad judgment, the adults got Gramps into our yellow Dodge and my father drove off, relying on Gramps for directions to the nearest hospital. The women remained, Grandma and Mommy sitting austerely on the sofa, my sister and I sprawled on the floor. The afternoon sun streamed through the closed windows until the house was stifling. Four of us strained against the forces of nature, praying for the impossible.

"Can't we *please* play a game?" I asked, trying to break the tension. It was my grandfather inside of me who was restless, who knew that waiting would make no difference. A game redeems all idleness. The silence continued for a minute and then my mother said, "You can go get a game."

I stepped over the backgammon board, opened for Gramps and best left untouched. Out on the porch I found a three-dimensional version of tic-tac-toe whose pieces rattled obtrusively as I lifted the box. Three clear plastic squares stacked on thin legs, unstable on top of the wall-to-wall carpeting. The sun lighted on dust motes in the air and shone bluntly through the layered panes. Black and red checker pieces felt too light in my palm. I tossed them around, placing them randomly on the clear high-rise. I knew no one would play with me.

Forever passed, and then the phone rang. Gramps had passed out in the car. My father, lost, had flagged down a tow truck that flashed its lights and raced through stop signs down Genesee Street. Gramps died shortly after they arrived at the hospital. My mother hung up the phone in the kitchen and conveyed this news to us with her hands limp at her sides. The medical staff harvested his eyes, she said. Pa wanted that, she said. Her tears began as the message sank in. Grandma wept softly on the sofa. I dismantled my transparent, sunlit tower, wondering what would happen to Gramps' eyes when they were no longer inside of his body.

Prayer is rarely what we expect. At first there's Venus, but then the whole house begins to emerge. The wall facing the east windows now exists; it looms and shifts, lighter than the north and south walls by a single degree. The change is so gradual, I don't notice until it's happened. The doorway to the kitchen gains dimension, the glass covering artwork glows. I realize once again that I have a body and it is solid, my spine aches, my hands are pulsing. Is this prayer? From my back, I gaze up through the piano window and can extrapolate the whole morning sky beyond my rooftop. It's a broad, concave expanse arching over the city, suddenly silver, suddenly azure. Venus is gone. Or she is there, but I grieve her visible reminder, the beam from a lighthouse warning me of the coastline. This day I'm sailing on is a vast, heaving ocean.

Where, after all, are Gramps' eyes? As a girl, I imagined them inside the sockets of a young woman's face, formerly blind but given sight by a dead man. The world through his eyes (through any eyes at all) must have seemed stunning. Today I consider how mortality must have intruded on the periphery of her vision. Sight, for that woman and for those who look, however briefly, through the ends of things, puts light in the perspective of darkness. Death is a constant companion, but not an unwelcome one. What's conscious and growing seems blindingly bright. At any point, we can reel heels over head through nothingness, spilling our busy days into that place of utmost silence.

This is what I want in prayer and what I most fear. Prayer is a headlong plunge into the unknown; it is an ego death, a taste of the void. Every morning it is the same. The cavernous emptiness around me fills with light, my heart strains for its pulse to be heard by the world, words spiral in my head. As with the universe, so it is with prayer; before there is something there first must be nothing. I strive for openness, that spirit might make its wild and unwieldy entrance. I may never again feel the sensation of spinning backward, but occasionally—blessed moment!— my heart leaps. It fills the living room, indistinguishable from sunlight.

You know what hour it is, how it is full time now for you to wake from sleep. For salvation is nearer to us now than when we first believed; the night is far gone, the day is at hand. So the early Christians heeded Paul's words—the edge of existence was so close! For them there was no literal tomorrow. Without a future unraveling its mundane promises, proceeding with life must have seemed ludicrous. *Now* was all the time left for being merry. Why not cast off possessions and fling oneself into revelry?

But then time went on and on, and the end, as the believers perceived it (even as we perceive it now, scoffing at their naïveté), never came. Paul reprimanded his flock to return to work lest the pagans consider them lazy. God will appear at any moment, he said, but still, get on with things.

Scientists tell us that each ounce of matter in the universe has its origin at a single point, dense and explosive; the eyes in my skull are made of stardust. Perhaps the apostle Paul was right after all, and the opposite of carrying our genesis is also true: our end is part and parcel of every instant. What awaits us after death—salvation, or life after reincarnated life, or the composting humus of a grave—already has arrived, and we contain it in our bodies. In prayer, then, we sit with origins and end times. No wonder I fear prayer's free fall more than I long for it. No wonder my mind fills with chattering distraction.

Wakefulness isn't meant for a later date. Nor is wellness, nor "deliverance to a place of safekeeping," as the Greeks defined salvation. Our creative lives—the lives we've always wanted, full of gaiety and connection and the leaning weight of grief, lives straining toward potential and time fattened with intention—they are meant for now. Salvation is this sun warming my skin. Salvation is the halo of light that fills the earth's atmosphere every morning. Out of all that dark vacuity, another day is born. It's an immaculate conception.

The day is at hand. I rise. I blow out my candle, irrelevant with all this sunlight. Venus has long since been obliterated. In Western cultures she is the morning star, the bearer of light, the ruler of springtime. But in the East, the planet is male, autumnal, the color of death. Daytime arrives with Venus's demise. During my grandfather's memorial service, I swung my stockinged legs and doodled with a pew pencil on the cover of the church bulletin. I drew the place I imagined Gramps had gone, a cemetery with flowers and bluebirds and a spiky sun. The cross that marked my grandfather's grave said, "Quentin Fischer A Very Good Man."

If death is the ultimate emptiness, it is also the seat of ultimate creation. My candle's extinguished flame is another death from which morning expands in all directions. I stretch myself up then out, behind then before. I emerge from the cavity of prayer into my home and another ordinary day. In reality, Gramps was cremated, his ashes saved to stir with my grandmother's and scatter to the wind. His body will mingle with a body he loved. My prayer rises now in smoky wisps the same way I imagine their ashes will, released into the exquisite latticework of creation.

ACKNOWLEDGMENTS

I am indebted to the community that inspired, nourished, and helped birth both myself and this book. Foremost I thank Marcia Peck, Carolyn Crooke, and Terri Whitman, whose questions, suggestions, and unflagging faith sustained me from the start. I feel tremendous gratitude toward Christine Sikorski, my neighbor and writing colleague, who made an otherwise lonely process companionable. Thanks to Paulette Bates Alden for her sweeping suggestions regarding this manuscript, her encouragement through the publishing process, and her many hours of time. Her generosity is a great inspiration. Thanks as well to Larry Sutin for his incisive observations, and to Robert Hedin and the Anderson Center for the time, advice, and resources they lent me. Thanks to Scott Edelstein for his negotiating smarts, to Sarah Warner for being the first to take notice of these pages, and to David Shoemaker for his dedicated struggle with the title. I am grateful to the Loft Literary Center, the Jerome Foundation, and Jerod Santag for the career initiative grant and the planning it made possible. For my many students, who have broadened my sense of the essay's form and purpose, as well as my clients, who have modeled for me the breadth of spiritual exploration, I give thanks. Many of these essays originally appeared (in an abbreviated form) in the Prospect Park United Methodist Church newsletter, *The*

Prospectus. Thanks to that congregation for being an engaging and forgiving audience. I ask the pardon of the friends and neighbors who appear in these pages with slightly altered identities and humbly thank them for thinking kindly of me regardless. In particular, I thank Barb Strom, Jared Cruz, Cil Braun, Stu Anderson, Dave Robinson, Linny Mae Siems, and especially Frank Carlson, who passed along to me a well-loved home. I also thank Kristen Blue, who got written out of this book but helped shaped these stories and the thought behind them. She is present throughout these pages.

I remain awestruck by the love and support given me by Emily Hughes. The intersection of her life with my own has filled this work with spirit. As always, much love to Helen, Len, and Marcy Andrew, who are my strong and trustworthy foundation. And a final thanks to Rhia, who curls up between my computer and the window and has kept me company during the many years of writing this book.